THE TALE OF

TWO GREAT CITIES

To Sharon

THE TALE OF

TWO GREAT CITIES

My Footballing Journey

Enjoy the Book

[signature]

Chris Jones

Published by Mylesiris Publishing

A CIP catalogue record for this book is available from the British Library.

ISBN 978-0-9930905-0-9 (Paperback)
ISBN 978-0-9930905-1-6 (Hardback)

Book layout and design by Clare Brayshaw

Prepared and printed by:

York Publishing Services Ltd
64 Hallfield Road
Layerthorpe
York YO31 7ZQ

Tel: 01904 431213

Website: www.yps-publishing.co.uk

DEDICATION

To the girls in my life – Therese, Sheriden, Francesca and Calista.

To Bill, as none of this would have happened without him.

The moving finger writes; and, having writ,
Moves on: nor all thy Piety or Wit
Shall lure it back to cancel half a Line,
Nor all thy Tears wash out a Word of it.

Omar Khayyam (*The Rubaiyat of Omar Khayyam* 1048-1131)

CONTENTS

PROLOGUE

It is just over 125 years since the formation of the Football League.

The first evidence of a football match came in around 1170, a hundred years after Omar Khayyam was writing his famous poetry.

In 1280 came the first account of a "kicking ball game". These games were usually violent, had no rules and often were banned. In 1280 at Ashington in Northumberland came an account of a player being killed as a result of running into an opposing player's dagger. No red card, just red blood.

William Fitzstephen wrote of his visit to London. "After dinner all the youth of the City goes out into the fields for the popular game of ball." He went on to say that each trade had its own team.

"The elders, the fathers and the men of wealth came on horseback to view the contests of their juniors and in their fashion sport with the young men and there seems to be aroused in these elders a stirring of natural heat by viewing so much activity and by participation in the joys of unrestrained youth."

No police, stewards or health and safety restrictions controlled "the stirring of natural heat" amongst the fans in those days.

It got a lot worse in 1314 when, through his worship the Lord Mayor of the City of London, Edward II of England had a decree issued about the game of football and the use of footballs. "Certain tumults arise from great footballs in the fields of the public from which many evils may arise." So football hooliganism was with us even in those days. The decree banned football from the City on pain of imprisonment for the perpetrators.

In 1581 came the first description of an organised football match, by a Richard Mulcaster a student at Eton College where he refers to teams ("sides"), positions ("standings") a referee ("judge over the parties") and a coach ("training master").

The first direct references to scoring a goal came from England in the 17th century. A poem by Michael Drayton in 1613 refers to "when the Ball to throw, and drive it to the goal, in squadrons forth they goe".

The concept of a football team is mentioned by the 17th century English poet Edmund Waller:

> *A company of lusty shepherds try*
> *Their force at football , care of victory...*
> *They ply their feet and still the restless ball,*
> *Tossed to and fro, is urged by them all.*

Football continued to be outlawed in the major cities; for example, the Manchester Lete Role contained a resolution dated October 12 1608: "... that where there hath been heretofore great disorder in our towne of Manchester, and the inhabitants thereof greatly wronged and charged with making and amending of their glasse windows broken yearly and spoyled by a company of lewd and disordered persons using that unlawful exercise of playing with the footeball in ye streets of said town. Therefore we of this jurye doe order that in future no manner of persons shall play or use the footeball in any street within the said towne of Manchester".

However despite tumults and various evils the game remained a gentleman's sport until 1848 when the first set of rules were drawn up by various Varsity men who formed "The Cambridge Rules". Various other bodies drew up their own rules but in 1863 they were moulded into one set of rules and the Football Association was formed.

In 1867 a loose offside rule was introduced that permitted forward passing and C W Alcock became noted as the first footballer ever to be ruled offside in a game in 1866. In the late 1860s team play and ball strategies started to evolve which led to the creation of the modern game as we know it.

In the 1860's the headmaster of Uppingham School the Reverend Edward Thring encouraged the playing of football. He saw it as an antidote to certain unhealthy activities amongst the boys which were believed at the time to cause physical weaknesses. "The mind boggles." The good Reverend hoped that the playing of football would encourage "manly attributes" which he believed were prevalent in the sport. It is rumoured that the boys carried on playing football as well. In the late 1880s football as a gentleman's game played by amateurs for the love of the game was coming to an end.

The first organised league came about in March 1888.

The founder was William McGregor, the Club Secretary of Aston Villa. He sent his famous letter to clubs suggesting that, "ten or twelve of the most prominent clubs in England combine to arrange home and away fixtures each season."

The first games were played on the 8th September 1888.

Preston's "Invincibles" were the first champions of England. They won 18 and drew four out of their 22 games. In 1891 a Liverpool engineer John Alexander Brodie invented the football net and as a centre forward I would be for ever grateful to him as I always dreamed of scoring goals and "hitting the back of the net".

The day of the old school tie and amateurism was about to come to an end and money and player power came to the fore.

In 1885 the Football Association permitted professionalism to the chagrin of William McGregor who deplored it. Transfer fees began to be paid by clubs.

Shortly afterwards, football's first major scandal was in the offing and about to make newspaper headlines.

In 1895 the former League Treasurer and Preston North End's Manager and Chairman, Major William Sudell, was sent to prison for embezzlement (he had used the League's money to fund the Club).

Ah well! Some things never change.

So this is football, and this is my story.

Chris Jones
York, December 2014

THE PARK AND THE STREET

It was a cold, dank November day in Altrincham in the early 1950s. The youngster, as yet nobody in particular, just a little boy bearing the name of Chris, was playing football with his Uncle Bill in Stamford Park. This is the first thing I can remember about myself and so I date the birth of my footballing odyssey from that cold, wet November morning.

The park in the days, just after the Second World War, was the centre of the universe for men young and old, and for every youngster who fancied himself as a Stanley Matthews, Billy Wright or Tom Finney. Men who had returned from the war with awful memories released tensions playing football. On occasion there may have been up to 20 on each side, the pitch becoming larger as the numbers swelled and the pile of coats and overalls that were the goal posts grew ever larger.

Most of the men and young adults who played (if they had a job) came from the big industrial areas in Atlantic Street, Broadheath, about two miles from Stamford Park. Linotype, a print setting firm, and Churchill's Machine Company were just two of the big employers found down Atlantic Street in Broadheath.

Broadheath was the first industrial estate in the world from 1885 to the mid 50s. That was because of the Bridgewater Canal and the nearness to Manchester for its industrial outlets. Trafford Park followed a year later in 1886 (close to "the old enemy" at Old Trafford).

Everybody arrived at the park on bikes, racing in like the finish of the Tour de France as they poured along Manchester Road, Barrington Road and Stamford New Road, over Moss Lane Bridge and down into the park via Moss Lane into a racing finish at the park gates.

We knew from the park when the main group were arriving, as coming out time at work was always started by the air-raid siren heralding the end of work for the day in Atlantic Street. We knew the game was going to be enlarged within 15 minutes. Depending on the time of year we may just get half an hour in for a game but it did not matter as we sometimes carried on in near darkness. Tea at home depended on when the game ended.

Stamford Park had been donated to Altrincham Borough by Lord Stamford in1880. It still is a 16 acre park, partly in Altrincham and partly in Hale with the dividing line being a duck pond. Over the fence on one side of the middle green was the duck pond, still there to this day, and many was the time the ball was kicked over the fence to the cries of, "don't let it go in the water". This was for a couple of reasons: somebody was going to have to wade for it, and once the leather ball with its lace and pig's bladder was wet only the brave or stupid could kick it. Even the many layers of dubbin failed to keep the ball in a kickable condition.

On the other side of the middle green was the bowling green with its doyens of the park. The gently domed crown green was hallowed land and woe betide anybody who allowed the football to encroach onto the sacred turf. It was generally patrolled by the legendary park keeper Alistair Gough. Alistair was a great crown green bowls player, but also, to those who frequented Stamford Park, the Manager of its most successful team – Stamford Lads. Any young player who thought he could play wished to be considered for this team, and as a young boy idolised any player who was known to play for the Lads

However that part of my young life was still in the future and a young boy's dreams still had to be tempered with the realities of life after the war, where rationing and ration books were still part of everyday life and central heating, indoor toilets and double glazing a long way in my future.

So my world of growing up was one of many happy times, probably sheltered from the stark reality of family survival by my uncle Bill and his sister Hazel, who sacrificed many things I did not know about at the time to give me a chance to make a start in life which most boys would envy. My dad Lister (Lea) had five children, two older sisters born before the war, myself and a brother and sister after the war. My mother I never knew and I and my elder sisters were brought up in my uncle's and aunt's house from my earliest memories. My grandmother Jesse was still alive until 1951 and was the matriarch of the family – a good, caring and formidable woman who herself was widowed early and had to bring up six children in a small terraced house in Hamon Road.

Her answer when her husband died in 1930 to a question about grief was, "I have no time to grieve, I have six children to bring up," a very pragmatic approach to life which I am sure my Uncle Bill thought about when taking me to live with him in 1948. My earliest recollection of my new home is having to share a bed with my two uncles, Myles (Bill) and Gordon, with frost developing on the inside of the window's. Somebody had to go down and light the damper to light the fire while the rest cowered under the blankets. We had an outdoor toilet (freezing to walk out into the yard and scary after dark) and no central heating. We had peat and coal delivered and that was tipped into our cellar and we had to go down in the dark with a candle as the gas mantle needed to be lit. Electricity we did not have in the early years after the war. However they did not seem to be hardships at the time but a normal way of life for a lot of ordinary families trying to come to terms with life after the war. There always seemed to be warmth and food on the table.

In a way, the war had been kind to my family. My grandmother's four sons joined up in 1939 and returned home unharmed in 1945. They joined the Cheshire Yeomanry regiment which was part of the 6th Cavalry Division and remained mounted until 1942. Bill, Gordon and Lea were in one of the last regiments of the British Army to fight on horseback in the cavalry in modern warfare in Palestine. They took part in the invasion of Syria, then held by the Vichy French, and had the distinction of taking part in the last cavalry charge by the British Army.

They lost their mounts in Palestine and Uncle Gordon, who was bugler, had to re-enrol in the Signals in 1942 and saw further action in the Western Desert and North West Europe. Two of my uncles' horses were named Stardust and Blackie and when I asked, "What happened to them when you joined the Signals?" they broke down and cried. Unlike *Warhorse* the fate of horses left by the cavalrymen had not a happy ending. Bill just said, "Don't ever ask me, Stardust was a great horse but it was too expensive to repatriate him and I do not want to think what happened to him."

In Palestine, Uncle Bill played for the Signals Regiment for Bury in the 1943-44 season in the Sarafand and District FA Division Three. My father, Lea, was assigned as a despatch rider and responsible for carrying penicillin hundreds of miles through the night to various outposts which could not be reached by air transport.

His other (unofficial) duty was to get Uncle Bill to places like Lydda (now Lod) to play football against the Lydda police (Blackburn Rovers).

Records say they won the Levant Cup and were runners-up in the League. Not even for a World War did the British troops stop playing football. My uncle always remembered Major Verdin, the President of the Sarafand League who gave his name to Verdin Grammar School, one of our Cheshire football rivals at Lymm Grammar School in the late 50s.

Percy, the eldest, served out the war in Bristol as every effort was made to avoid a whole generation of a family being wiped out. Perhaps in a way this made up for my grandfathers' death in 1930 from the effects of gas inhaled when taking munitions by horse to the French on the front line in France in 1917. He was decorated by the French with the Medaille d'Honneur for his conspicuous bravery but finally paid the ultimate price with his demise from the gas he inhaled.

He was part of the Royal Garrison Artillery 31st Siege Battery in France from 1915 and was responsible for firing howitzers and storing munitions. My Grandfather was born in Walmsley, a Chapelry in Bolton le Moor in 1885 and married my Grandmother Jesse Hope Hemingway in October 1911. He was baptised at Christchurch and lived locally in Sharples in his early life. That may be why Uncle Bill always took me to watch Bolton Wanderers in my early years rather than the big Manchester clubs.

When we were not taking the buses necessary to get us to Burnden Park, home of Bolton Wanderers, known as the Trotters, we were following the fortunes of Altrincham Football Club known as the Robins.

Altrincham Association Football Club originated at the Rigby Memorial School on Stamford Road on Broadheath Bridge and started life as Broadheath AFC in 1903. The ground was built on what was known as Hale Moss back in June 1903, although it is thought that the Club could date back to 1891.

In those days of the 50s and 60s Bolton Wanderers were in the First Division while Altrincham were in the Cheshire League.

The first footballer I tried to emulate was Nat Lofthouse, fearless striker for Bolton and England. Every move Nat made in the early days I tried to copy when we returned to the park, practising endlessly the skills he had to create a chance to score. Yes, even from those early days I only dreamed of goal scoring.

Back at Altrincham they had many players who graced the Robins ground in the late 50s and early 60s such as Ernie Taylor, Charley Mitten, Walter Jones and Jackie Swindells. The latter was a prolific goal scorer who scored 62 goals in 63 games in two seasons at the Club and always took the eye, as did my namesake Walter Jones, a giant of a centre forward who also played for Rochdale Hornets at rugby league.

Over Moss Lane Bridge in Cross Street there was a sheet music publisher's, run at the time by the little known Noel White and Peter Swales. My sisters used to take me in to look at the latest chart music. White and Swales started in 1951 and had many shops all over Cheshire by the time they took over the running of Altrincham Football Club in 1961. By then they had diversified and were into television rentals and owned the Bowdon Hotel.

Noel White spent many years as Director at Altrincham Football Club before joining the Board of Liverpool FC. Both Peter Swales and Noel White became heavily involved on the Football Association's ruling bodies and committees.

Later, Noel White and David Dein of Arsenal were responsible for brokering the deal leading to the formation of the Premier League in 1992.

So my early years all revolved round Stamford Park. On one side was Stamford Park Primary where I went to school, Altrincham Football Club at Moss Lane and our house in Hamon Road on the other sides of the Park. We lived in a two bedroom terraced house in the road with an entry to the side. The other half of Hamon Road is now part of the Tesco supermarket chain and any similarity to the fifties has been buried by the avalanche of time and the march of progress.

The entry to the side of our house in Hamon Road was about ten yards wide and 20 yards long with back yards and corrugated roofs all the way down one side. At the end was a street light and many was the evening we played football with the bins as goals at each end of the entry. Anybody who has seen the John Smith's advert on television where they kick the ball into the air and it bounces on the corrugated roof can picture what happened often in our road. We used to wait until it stopped bouncing and came to rest in somebody's yard before sending my brother Philip over the wall to retrieve it. It was always my brother as you either had to be daft or courageous or both to hop over some person's wall and defy the wrath of a person with a stick. On occasion there was a dog lying dormant in a kennel waiting to pounce on an unsuspecting trespasser and the art of getting in and out without leaving part of your anatomy behind ("behind" being just the word).

So life in the fifties took its course with me attending primary school and with my uncle taking me everywhere, encouraging me to play all sports especially swimming, cricket and football.

Football was always our first love and like most boys I dreamed of becoming a professional footballer and running out at the big grounds and scoring lots of goals. The thought of money was never in my mind in those days, but you dreamed of the adulation of the fans and that always spurred me on. Roy of the Rovers is mentioned nowadays by television pundits, but to boys growing up it was the must-read and enhanced my dreams of following in the footsteps of my football idols.

THE GRAMMAR SCHOOL

Olim Meminisse Juvabit
One day it will be a joy to remember.

This is the word that year by year,
While in her place the school is set,
Every one of her Sons must hear,
And none that hears it dare forget.
This they all with a joyful mind
Bear through life like a torch in flame,
And falling fling to the host behind –
"Play up! Play up! And play the game!"

Vitae Lampada – The torch of Life – Sir Henry Newbolt

In 1956 the academic part of my life suddenly came to the fore and football had to take a backward step. The Eleven-Plus was upon me. Was I to pass to a Grammar school or end up across the road at Bradbury Central?

I was asked to make my choices in case I passed and was given three Grammar schools to choose from, Altrincham, Sale and Lymm. My choice was Altrincham, being a good football school. Sale was my third choice as they played rugby and I would rather have ended up across the road from Stamford Park Primary at Bradbury Central (no longer there).

Lymm Grammar was a football school going co-Educational, a very old school full of tradition but way out in the Cheshire countryside. When the results came out a relieved but scared youngster found himself passing the Eleven-Plus but condemned to a daily bus ride out to Lymm..

So my secondary school life began in 1956 and at Lymm football was still king. My reputation as a good football player seemed to have preceded me and within two weeks I found myself playing not for my year group but the under 13 team at Chester Kings Grammar School. I would like the reader to think that I scored the winning goal on my debut but the truth was that we were annihilated 10-0.

However, my first season at my own age group was successful: we won all six games, including a memorable 6-5 over the old enemy Altrincham Grammar School. No matter what level of football I played at through the years, a derby match was always special and that was my first taste of what it meant not just for the team, but for the whole school. As sports people say, we had bragging rights until next time.

So the school football, cricket and cross country became a way of life at school mixed in with the minimum amount of academic work. I had to maintain a fine balance as I did not want to lose my football to school detentions, which were on Saturday mornings as were our football fixtures.

During the winter I also did some cross country running, not because I loved the sport but because I believed the stamina and speed involved would improve my chances of fulfilling my dreams of becoming a professional footballer.

The cross country was interesting as we went quite a way out from the school. For those who know the Lymm area, we used to go down Oughtrington Lane, under the Bridgewater Canal and up on to its banks, along to Mill Lane under the canal and then a circuit through Spud Wood nearby and then back along what is now the Mersey Valley Trail and back into school at Oughtrington Cricket Club. It was about four and a half miles for those who completed the course and a nice relaxing outing for one or two character's who stopped on the river bank near Spud Wood for a quiet 'fag'. In summer I played cricket in the junior's team at Timperley Cricket Club.

Bolton Wanderers were always my Uncle Bill's favourite club and I was excited in March 1957 when he said we were going to Old Trafford to see Bolton Wanderers open the new floodlights in a League game against Manchester United.

It was a great night as Bolton won 2-0. My biggest memory, however, was the all red strip of United and the glistening all white kit of Bolton Wanderers (changed from white with black shorts for the occasion). I was also privileged to see two great centre forwards in Nat Lofthouse and Tommy Taylor in action, a real thrill for an 11 year old.

Sad that Tommy, along with the other Busby Babes, should die so tragically less than a year later in the Munich air crash.

So the early years at school rolled on while I kept playing for the school, and at every game hoping that some scout from a professional club would recognise my abilities.

In the late fifties and early sixties, the clubs never had schools of excellence and academies for young footballers; trying to be "discovered" became the bane of my young life. Frustratingly, I was hearing about the Stockport and Manchester Boys teams and how these players looked to be future apprentices at the big clubs.

Down in the sleepy Cheshire countryside I felt that my football career would never take off. My school also played football matches throughout Cheshire and from a school in Winsford I had heard about a centre forward who not only played for Mid-Cheshire Schools but also had been selected for England Schoolboys at Wembley. I had never even been put forward for trials for Cheshire Schools and felt let down by my school. My mates had begun to scoff at my dreams, but disappointed and chagrined as I was deep down I was determined to fulfil my dream.

The player who was at school in Winsford, Cheshire was Glyn Pardoe, who was later my strike partner in the Manchester City Youth team and became and still is a very good friend.

Inter-mingled with school was still the park where at weekends if I was not playing in a team I was practising every skill I could pick up from the Bolton Wanderers team whom we watched. Life became a whirl of football, from playing for the school on Saturday morning, for the Lads in the afternoon and a team called Timperley Athletic on a Sunday afternoon. My reason for playing for Timperley Athletic was purely selfish as I knew they played in the Manchester League and that brought me into the Stockport and Manchester areas where I hoped scouts may be looking for talent.

My one acknowledgement as a young player was to be selected for the Altrincham and Sale Boys team at the age of 14 and I remember playing at Linotype's football ground in Broadheath, Altrincham. The only memorable things about that game were that we played it in a snowstorm, won 3-2 and I scored a couple of goals. Again nothing happened to further my football dreams and another season passed at school.

Junior football games, more practice and still more derision from so called mates who did not share my ambition.

STAMFORD LADS

These early years round Stamford Park were happy times and Stamford Lads had a very good young side that won all before them in the Altrincham Junior League, except for two particular games – the ones against Manchester United Juniors.

For most readers used to the modern game it would be hard to believe that these two sides could ever meet, yet the most awaited game on the park was "Lads v Man United." The ground would be roped off for the big game and fresh lime was put out to mark the pitch. The Juniors would always arrive kitted out to play while the Lads changed in the air-raid shelter by the side of the pitch, with no light and only a bucket of water to wash off afterwards.

I was there a while ago and the hut is now the groundsman's hut. Oh yes, I forgot to mention the ground: it was mainly scrub grass down the sides and dried out soil for the rest of it. The game was always a nightmare for the goalkeepers who always wore track suit bottoms. Still it was a tremendous spectacle for the locals who used to encroach round the ground three deep, hoping for a glimpse of a future star in the making. I never found out the feelings of the Manchester United Juniors who had to play on such a surface but it was always a good close match and they played for a few years in that league.

Playing for the Lads at that time was a young full back called Peter Leigh, who was signed on as a professional for Manchester City and went on to become a distinguished player for Crewe Alexander. Peter was to make 473 appearances for Crewe and had a testimonial match against Manchester City in 1967. I was privileged to play in that game for a truly top League professional. I never saw a lot of Peter, although I should have as he lived in the same road as me and occasionally joined in the kickabouts in the yard.

It amazes me to look back and realise how certain twists of fate put you on the road to what you become. Jimmy Greaves said: "Football's a funny old game", and no truer words have been spoken.

All my attempts to be discovered never worked and yet a few doors away from me lived the person who very slightly opened a door which would lead me to achieve my football ambitions. I was too shy a person to ask Peter Leigh about his football success and had to ask my family to enquire how to get a trial at the football Club.

Two weeks after the enquiry was made Peter passed a message back that Manchester City were having an Open trial at their Chassen Road training ground in Urmston and that if I was interested to go to the ground on the Saturday and register to play in the trial.

This was it: a chance to maybe prove to everybody that I was a good footballer. All sorts of emotions went through me during that week leading to the day of the trial. This was the close season, the month of June, I think. I was still going to school every day but my mind on only one thing: the football trial. The thought of failure on the Saturday haunted me: was this my last chance to fulfil my dream? Was I going to have to go back and face my mates as an abject failure? Whatever happened, I must not have an injury during the week and be ready when my chance came to go through all the skills which I had practised on the Park over all those years. Friday night before the trial was a nervous affair for me but my Uncle Bill always believed I could "play a bit".

It was on the Friday night when we had our talk and set out how I was going to play. I was going to put myself down as a centre forward. The aim was to go through all the basic skills, good passing, use of two feet, once having passed the ball move into space and if a chance came to shoot then I must take the shot.

THE FOOTBALL TRIAL

Niti, querere, et invenire non cedere.
To strive, to seek, to find and not to yield.

A sleepless night on Friday was followed by an equally nervous Saturday morning. My uncle, I realised later, was going through all sorts of emotion as my failure would upset him deeply – Not so much for himself but he lived his life in those years just to help me be a success and my ambitions were his.

Saturday morning dragged slowly; I checked my kit endlessly, looking at the boots making sure the stud length was right and the studs tight, checking the rest of the kit – shirt, shorts, socks, spare studs and a towel; nothing could be left to chance.

One eye was always on the clock as I nervously waited for the time to go over Moss Lane Bridge, catch the 47 bus to Stretford and then the Manchester bus to Flixton and Urmston.

I had what I thought was a football meal consisting of steak and toast. The butcher around the corner heard I was having a trial for Manchester City and gave me a fillet steak for nothing, a really nice gesture.

Time to leave the house! That was the hardest step. My Aunt Hazel looked nervous but Bill tried to put on a calm, confident face. Once under way the journey became one of bursts of nervous talk and long silences.

We both knew there was nothing to say: once at the ground it was all down to me. We knew what I had to do and it was a time to concentrate solely on this football trial. How I arrived at Chassen Road I will never know.

When I arrived and saw the ground I became overawed by the mass of footballing humanity in front of me. I was later to find out that the number of trialists had exceeded 100.

At that moment my heart sank and I never felt such a low point in my life. How was I ever going to impress anybody amongst this number? For one moment I was ready to turn around and go home. I looked at Bill, remembered my mates laughing at what I wanted to achieve and thought of all I had gone through over the years to reach this point. An old saying of my family came to mind at that moment *Better we have tried and failed than never tried at all.* With that resolve I entered the changing area where the players had formed long queues to register age and position. Three columns: one for defence and goalkeepers, one for the midfield players and one for the wingers and forwards. I joined the latter queue and waited patiently for my turn.

The person patiently writing down names and positions had a small booklet which I had noticed he kept flicking from page to page as one player after another gave his name and position and went to get ready for the trials. In this book the registrar had a page for each position and as I got closer I realised centre forward was the most popular position. When I got close enough to see the book wingers seemed to be in short supply.

When it was finally my turn, the person wearily asked name and position and on the spur of the moment I said, "Chris Jones and I play right wing." I think on looking back my one thought was that I would get more of a game in that position and have more time to impress. However at the time it was all against our carefully laid plans. The rest of the afternoon was quite a blur. After we were all changed we were put into teams and started with a game lasting about fifteen minutes, and then players were switched in and out and this continued for about an hour. I think I played two halves, both in my right wing position.

I played as Bill and I planned, good control, good passing, moving into space to receive a pass and when I had to deliver two corners I used my left foot to deliver one of them.

I then came off and had to watch a further half hour of trials. Meanwhile some players had arrived and they turned out to be the apprentice professionals and signed amateurs. Since my name had been called out to play in the trial nobody had talked to me and watching the game I became disillusioned at what was happening and told my uncle I was going to get changed. This I did and came back out ready to go. At this point I noticed the apprentices were warming up and the word was they were going to play the last trial against the final trialists.

This was too much for me and I said to Bill, "Let's go." I am eternally grateful that he replied: "Let's just see what the standard is like from those who have been selected."

Disconsolately I agreed and leaned on the rail near the changing room to watch a lady supporter who always came to watch juniors and young players walk by. She said to a dapper man in a smart suit and trilby, "Have you found any players today Harry?" and the reply came from a few yards behind me.

"Yes and I have bloody lost him."

Still I was not interested until the lady, God bless her, said, "What's his name?" Came the reply:

"Chris Jones."

I jumped as I swung round.

"I'm Chris Jones."

To this day I can hear his reply. "What are you doing here changed? You are supposed to be playing in this trial." In moments I was in my kit and out on the pitch, playing right wing for the half hour.

Again I played the game simply and at the end went with the rest of the trial team into a dressing room and told to wait.

Some of the group talked nervously and we were wondering what was happening. Some wise person said they were deliberating on who was going to be kept and those who were not going to be selected. After 20 minutes of nerve jangling intensity the man in the trilby who introduced himself as Harry Godwin came in and read out six names to go out for a talk with him. My name was not read out and my heart sank. I looked around at the four remaining players.

Vaguely I thought that those who were left were good players but none of us was looking confident. Eventually Harry Godwin returned and also the man with the little book who I was to find out was John

Hart, a legendary player in the fifties. We were put out of our misery straight away and Harry Godwin said he would like us to come down training at Chassen Road on Tuesdays and Thursdays nights at 6.15.

Sheer elation was an understatement and swelling with pride I could not wait to get outside and talk to Bill patiently waiting for the result. I think looking back he may have gathered that I was successful, but you are never sure.

In the still of the early evening Bill and me looked out over a now quiet Chassen Road and contemplated the greatest success in my young footballing life.

The noise of so many young players striving for success had now gone. Bill, whom always loved his poetry and recited various quotes to me over the years, was at this time speechless but I am sure very proud. However I could remember words from one of the poems.

All I could hear in my mind were the words from *Recessional* by Rudyard Kipling, which Bill liked.

The tumult and the shouting dies –
The Captains and the Kings depart –
Still stands Thine ancient sacrifice,
An humble and a contrite heart.

Yes I had come through the trial but a lot of footballers with the same dreams had them shattered that day. We both enjoyed that Saturday as did my Aunt Hazel and all the family. For me however this trial was only the beginning and we all knew that the hard work and the trials and tribulations of growing up in a football world had only just begun.

The time of Stamford Park and 'the Lads' was now over and I looked forward to a new level of coaching and experience with Jonny Hart, Dave Ewing, Dick Neilson and Harry Godwin at Manchester City Football Club.

SIGNING AMATEUR FOR MANCHESTER CITY

Those Summer days of 1962 flew by. I was training on Tuesdays and Thursdays at the training ground, getting a lot fitter and learning all about how to play the game in a professional environment.

During those months I was never asked to sign as an Amateur and was becoming concerned that maybe any day the Club was going to say I was not good enough and ask me not to come training. I kept seeing players who were signed Amateur collect expenses on a Thursday night and wondered what would happen when training stopped at Chassen Road and moved to Maine road.

Maine Road, home of Manchester City Football Club, at that time far away and just a dream in my heart that one day I would be there playing football. Other than the odd training session where the Apprentices were training with us we had no real contact with the professional game and even Glyn Pardoe who was my age had already made his first team debut and was a distance away from my life.

October came and was nearly gone when the word came that training was to end at Chassen Road on the following Tuesday and the signed players were going to be training from then on at Maine Road. My heart sank and still not a confident individual I went home on that Tuesday evening with a feeling of dread.

Nobody had talked to me about what was to happen to me and for the following 48 hours I put myself through all sorts of mental tortures. Was my dream coming to an end? The Thursday was the last training session and I decided that I had to pluck up courage and talk to Harry Godwin the chief scout and put myself out of my misery. My courage failed me and I trained that evening as best as I could. After the session John Hart and Harry Godwin called for a quick meeting to explain what was going to happen the following week when the players were to decamp to Maine Road. I sat disconsolate amongst about fifteen players wondering if this was to be the end of the road for my football life. The signed players left, leaving me last in the dressing room and at that moment with only Harry Godwin left in the dressing room I spurted out to Harry, "What's going to happen to me, Harry?", and back came the reply, "Oh Chris, we are signing you next week as an Amateur, see you at Maine Road, half past six next Tuesday, don't be late".

Another great moment in my life, the dream was to go on and I was going to sign as an Amateur at my own theatre of dreams, Maine Road. A more mundane problem crossed my mind at the time, how to get to the ground for training as the days of owning a car were far away.

The following Tuesday the 1st December 1962 according to an old forgotten diary was the day I was going to sign the forms to play for Manchester City. It took an age to come round and when it did it proved to be a cold murky day and evening in the Manchester area.

To get to Maine Road on that Tuesday night I had to get the Electric train from Altrincham to Oxford Road in Manchester and then a bus out to Moss Side either dropping me on Claremont Road or Platt Lane depending on the number of bus which passed first.

As it turned out the bus dropped me at Princess Parkway and by then the cold dark day had turned into an evening 'pea souper', an industrial fog which put the Moss Side area into an eerie place to walk. Along Claremont Road and up Platt Lane I groped my way towards the football ground, very spooky and lonely with hardly a street light to guide me.

When I arrived I found only a little light on next to the main entrance and not a soul around. I knocked on this side door, waited a while and was pondering what to do next when the door opened and Dave Ewing loomed large in the doorway. "What are you doing here son, there is no training tonight?" he said in his Scots accent. I said in a very disappointed way, "I have come to see Mr Godwin and sign for the Club". Dave said that I would have to come back on the Thursday, and disconsolately as the door shut again I started to make my weary way back through the smog of Moss Side wondering if anything was ever going to happen easily for me.

I could hardly see my hand in front of me as I worked my way down Claremont Road and actually bumped into Harry Godwin going in the other direction to Maine Road. An amazing coincidence! Harry just said the weather had put off training and to come back on the Thursday to sign the forms.

I am sure that Harry always appreciated that meeting and gave him the felling that he was signing a very determined player. I in turn was hoping that the men who were giving me this chance in football would not be let down and that I would do all I could to become a very good player in the light blue colours of Manchester City.

The following Thursday I duly turned up and signed the amateur forms for Manchester City.

I was asked to sign for the first time for my expenses and to this day have kept the fifty shilling note that I received. I trained the following week and at the end of the Thursday training session was told that I was included in the Lancashire League B team game at Blackburn on the Saturday.

Throughout my career there was no greater thrill than that day when I pulled on the light blue Manchester City shirt for the first time. I played right-wing that day and scored my first goal in a 3-2 win.

Further games followed in the B team against Bury and Blackpool containing a mixture of apprentices and amateurs. Just before Christmas of 1962 John Hart said he wanted me to play centre forward.

I think he knew all along that this was my favoured position and that I had a knack for scoring goals.

The game was against Bolton Wanderers at Chassen Road and I was fortunate to score again. My Grandads' side Bolton Wanderers whom we supported as a youth kept cropping up throughout my career as opposition and seemed to be a side I could always score against at every level.

Manchester United at the Cliffe was always a tough game, a 'derby match' and one which got the adrenalin flowing more than normal.

This was my first view of a wisp of a winger who had a prodigious talent and in my opinion became the best player on the planet. Of course this player was George Best and on this day actually mesmerised our right back Mike Harold and I was glad I was at the other end of the field to George just admiring his pace, skill, ue of both feet and his finishing ability.

Christmas of 1962 was the start of the 'Big Freeze'. My small football diary with a very young boys notes on the footballing events suddenly dried up in December 1962.

For those who were too young or not born that was the winter when the whole of Football was shut down due to snow and bitter weather, which meant no football ground in the country was playable. It was one of the coldest winters on record with deep snow in most places followed by the country freezing solid with temperatures as low as -16°C and my old friend 'frozen smog' around the Manchester area.

No football was played from the end of December until 12th February 1963 when Everton managed to play a match. During that time Professional Clubs had attempted to beat the freeze, Blackpool had tried flame-throwers on the pitch, Chelsea tar burners and Leicester City a large tent all to no avail. The cold beat everybody.

My football career was put on hold, although we continued to train in the two gymnasiums under the stands at Maine Road. The football pitch at the ground was like concrete and even the running track round the pitch was too dangerous to use. In February we had a 36 hour blizzard, loads of snow and gale force winds up to 80 miles an hour.

Intrepid as ever we continued to train. It was a continuous round of circuit-training, weights, head-tennis and skittle ball.

Until early March it was a battle to get out to school in the Cheshire countryside (sometimes the buses made it and sometimes we were left stranded in Altrincham).

My trips to Maine Road were just as tortuous, buses were mainly running but some were cancelled and as I mentioned the freezing smog was awful and left sooty deposits when you blew your nose.

We finally came out of the 'Ice Age' in early March 1963. My first game for the Lancashire League 'B' team was on the 2nd March and we beat Blackburn 2-0 at Chassen Road.

The FA Cup 3rd round matches were finally completed by the middle of March, and the 'Old Enemy' Manchester United went on to win the Cup 3-1 against Leicester City.

City were having another indifferent season although my main concern in 1963 was to get my football career back on track and that meant playing well for the Lancashire League B team and signing on for another year.

The backlog of fixtures meant that we were playing until late April 1963 very unusual and an overlap into the cricket season. Games at Everton and Liverpool training grounds matches at Burnley and Blackpool, a return game against Manchester United at the Cliffe followed, George Best starring as we were hammered 7-0 and finally the season came to an end.

I was elated when told that I was to sign again the following season by Harry Godwin and went off to play some cricket at Timperley during the close season and complete my exams at Lymm Grammar School.

The school at this time was becoming a problem as they were not happy with my association with a Professional Football Club. At the time the school was changing to a more Rugby orientated school and I was continually at loggerheads with a new PE teacher Danny Harris a Welsh Rugby Union International.

The days of the football teachers had gone and threats of disrupting my football at Manchester City were growing as I was being pressured into playing Rugby for the school the following season. Luckily the summer holidays arrived and I was back into training in July at Urmston with Manchester City.

DIARY ENTRIES 1963

My diary entries for July, August and September 1963 can give an insight into the problems of a young boy trying to achieve a career in Football.

Training at Chassen Road on Tuesday – (tough training session with Jimmy Meadows)

Thursday 15th August – Trial Match

Saturday 17th August – Trial Match, played poorly (but not to be discouraged – keep going)

Thursday 22nd August – Trial Match (scored a hat-trick – George Poyser the manager watched it. (elated)

Saturday 24th August – Lost to Manchester United B 6-2 – played ok.

Tuesday and Thursday – training at Chassen Road.

Selected for Manchester City A at Preston, drew 0-0

3rd September – Training

4th September – watched Manchester City beat Cardiff 4-0 at Maine Road.

Thursday – Training

Saturday 7th September – played against Rochdale Reserves at Spotland – scored 2 goals. 500 spectators watched game.

14th September – Drew 2-2 with Bolton Wanderers A scored a goal.

Oldham A lost 2-1 – scored the goal. Lad broke leg in Oldham goal – clash with me. (Until this day I can still feel the impact from the challenge and though it was a complete accident, you do not as a player want to be involved in that sort of incident. The goalkeeper and me were just too brave on that occasion and if he had dived out instead of swinging a leg he would have been alright).

I returned to school the same week in September 1963 to do some re-sit exams. I was immediately threatened by the school that they were going to dismantle my opportunity in football by reporting Manchester City to the English schools FA. Rumour or fact I terminated my education at that point and I left school in October 1963.

I retained my place in the Manchester City A team through September and into October and then on a Thursday night the 10th October I was told I might make my debut in the Reserves at Maine Road. (I knew I had been getting good notices about my play and goal scoring in the A Team, but this came out of the blue).

I had to train on my own and at the end of the evening it was confirmed.

Excitement, nerves, everything imaginable went through me during that evening and it was hard to believe that I was going to play at Maine Road, and me still an amateur.

Diary entry for 12th October 1963 – Bolton Wanderers Reserves drew 1-1, played best ever game at centre forward. Up against Brian Edwards (a Bolton hero of mine). Scored with header in 61st minute. Signed many autographs.

Sunday 10th – Football is a great life. (I was starting to live a young boy's dream).

Mike Doyle was also in the team on that day and his quote when I Scored at the Platt Lane End as was always to be the case with my goals from 'Doyley', "lucky Grammar School 'Twat', it went in off your shoulder". My retort as always was "not how 'Doyley' but how many". Mike Doyle was always gracious to his team mates! Kept my place in the Reserve team the following week at Derby County and won 1-0.

We had a large Professional squad at Manchester City and it was nearly unheard of for an Amateur to be playing in the Reserves. However my diary entry for the 26th October shows the fickleness of the game and how it can change and how you can come down to earth with a bump.

Quote – not selected for the Reserves. A team have no game and picked for the B Team against Bury B. Played right-wing not centre forward, won 2-1, had a poor game. Already I was learning the 'ups and downs' of a footballers life and I wasn't even a Professional.

The following week I was told that I may be playing against Manchester United in the A Team but at the end of the evening was told I was travelling to Newcastle as Reserve for the Central League side at St. James Park, the pendulum had swung again.

At the time there were no substitutes as John Hart found out when playing in goal with a broken thumb at Bury.

It would be the 21st August 1965 when Keith Peacock became the first substitute when he replaced Mike Rose the Charlton goalkeeper in an away game at Bolton Wanderers. Bobby Knox became the first substitute to score a goal when he played for Barrow against Wrexham. A substitution was only allowed for injury and it would be 1967-68 before tactical substitutions were allowed.

Diary entry – Newcastle United – 3 hour journey, good food, poor game, loved atmosphere of great stadium, pity I didn't play.

However I was still an amateur with Manchester City and needed to get a job. I took on the position of a clerk at the gas board close to Stamford Park and for two months until Christmas I combined training at night with Manchester City, playing for the Club and working as a filing clerk. Football can bring you down very quickly and you have to have reality checks on what is happening to you now and then.

Meanwhile the Apprentices were still training and playing at Maine Road.

John Clay signed apprentice forms in July 1962. John I consider to have been the most gifted player in our Youth team. He had I discovered been selected for the Cheshire boy's side (the one I never heard about at Lymm Grammar) from Stockport Grammar School. However Mike Doyle reserved the 'Grammar School 'Twat' for me.

Also in the Cheshire side was Bobby Noble who would play against us in the Manchester United Youth team. Sadly for Bobby he crashed his car in Sale one evening and it shortened his career. I came along the same road just afterwards and was detoured. I only found out the following day who was in the accident.

Alfie Wood signed Full time Professional in 1962 along with Glyn Pardoe and they were the only members of the future youth team to break into the first team during the relegation season of 1962-63.

That was the year when Alex Harley managed to score 23 goals in a failing season.

In April 1962 Glyn made his debut as Manchester City's youngest player while at the same time I was sat in a classroom only thinking about how to get a trial for a Professional club. Glyn like most of the younger players had difficulty getting to training and had to use a bus and train to get from Winsford in Cheshire and extra buses if the training was at Chassen Road.

Nothing was easy for young players like me in those days and travelling to training by circuitous routes was a way of life. After a couple of months at the Gas Board working by day and training at night something had to give and my Uncle Bill told me to leave. Another sacrifice from him as he would have to subsidise me for a while and less money would come into the household. For working people this I realised was a serious step and to continue feeding another mouth on small incomes was a great sacrifice while I tried to further my ambition to make Football as a career.

However this did give me the opportunity to train with the young professionals and Apprentices at Maine Road and was a great help in moulding myself into the Youth team and also becoming a lot fitter. I was also under the eye of Johnny Hart, Jimmy Meadows, Harry Godwin and George Poyser which I hoped would lead into a Professional contract.

Mike Doyle who signed Apprentice forms in May 1962. A very good player was Mike who was good in the air but at the time of the Youth matches found himself playing Right-Back. It was only under Malcolm Allison that he played a few games at Centre Forward before forming his partnership with George Heslop at the centre of Manchester City's defence. He disliked Manchester United intensely and for some reason had a running feud with George Best from the early years of the Lancashire League, Central League and of course the Youth Cup semi-finals.

From my point of view I just admired the talent on show that was George Best and a privilege to have played against him in this era.

Bobby McAlinden signed in August 1962 and along with John Clay was the heart of mid-field. A left-footed payer was 'Mac' who complimented 'Cassius' and formed a very creative pairing at that time. He exasperated Dick Neilson who was the 'B' team trainer with some of his antics. We were playing Blackburn Rovers at Chorley one Saturday and Dick was not happy with our performance and wanted his say in the dressing room at half-time. Just as Dick started in with his team talk 'Macca' got out a couple of Mars bars and was tearing the wrapper off them. He started to bite on one and Dick nearly had epilepsy as he became speechless and Bobby unconcernedly chewed on it. We were quite happy for the distraction as we knew we were in for a lambasting from Dick. By the time he found some words to say Bobby was on his second bar and the team talk went out of the window. All Dick would say was "get out there and do better". And to Bobby, "you better not be sick". Well we got it together and came out of the game with a draw 'Macca' had a good second half and at the end we all asked Dick if Mars bars couldn't go with the half-time cup of tea in future. The answer is unrepeatable.

Ron Frost was signed apprentice in July 1962 and managed to break into the first team before me. Ron actually scored in a 4-3 defeat at the Valley against Charlton Athletic in mid-February 1964 and kept his place for the following game against Grimsby at Maine Road. That defeat against Grimsby 4-0 lost Ron his place on the wing and although we were to continue having success in the Youth team that was Ron's last match in Manchester City's first team.

David Wild who played left back in the Youth team is the saddest of stories. David had played so well that Phil Burrows (with me at York City) had to play in mid-field. Unfortunately for David the semi-final against Manchester United as it was for Mike Doyle was a disaster as both wing men John Aston and Willy Anderson took our full backs apart. David was not offered a Professional contract. He was always devoted to football and stayed in the game in non-league. David tragically died of a brain tumour at the young age of fifty.

Phil Burrows and Max Brown both got a year's professional contract with an option to renew but in 1966 neither player was kept on by Joe Mercer and Malcolm Allison. As Manchester City were heading back into the First Division I looked at the much heralded Youth side and discovered that there were only six of us left. Alan Ogley, Mike Doyle, Glyn Pardoe, Dave Connor, John Clay and me. At this time in 1966 I was scoring prolifically in the reserves but never got the call from Joe and Malcolm. It was getting increasingly difficult to forge a place in the team as both Mike Summerbee and Colin Bell had arrived and Neil Young was playing well as a striker if called on.

Alan Ogley our goalkeeper was transferred to Manchester City from Barnsley. He had already played 9 games for Barnsley and had signed for them in February 1963. At the end of the season George

Poyser signed him to challenge Harry Dowd for the goalkeeping position, although it was a bad time to come to Maine Road. The 'Old enemy' had just taken a point out of the club with a 1-1 draw and the 'sword of Damocles' hung over the club as relegation threatened.

David Connor who was an amateur but signed as a fulltime professional in December of 1962.

Dave was my mate at Maine Road and we had similar and fortuitous paths to Professional Football. He had an opportunity to go for a trial to Manchester United but it was on the same day as a trial for City at Chassen Road. Dave looked at the money in his pocket and found the bus fare would only go as far as Maine Road where he was to be picked up to go to Urmston by Johnny Hart. Going to the Cliffe would have left him out of pocket so Joe Armstrong at United lost a player more or less on the flip of a coin or more exactly the coin left in Dave's pocket.

On the Monday 4th November 1962 I was selected for the Youth Team against the Reserve team at Maine Road. My diary entry just said, good game, scored in 2nd half through Trautmann, score 5-4 to us.

Mike Doyle as I said could never keep his mouth shut and along with reminding Bert of his record number of goals conceded against Leicester City in 1958 had to also let Bert know after the first march of the 1962-63 season which they had lost by the score of 8-1 to Wolverhampton Wanderers.

An arrogant young Doyle had the nerve to say "Hi, Bert, how's the back". (relating to having to pick the ball out of the net eight times). Bert had to take a lot of jibes about who won the war but he was not about to take anything from a young whipper-snapper and grabbed him with one big fist and lifted him up and suspended him like an impaled crab of the dressing room 'peg' by his tracksuit top. I thought he could have looked like a paratrooper suspended from a tree as an analogy but I didn't say it and maybe suffer the same fate as 'Doyley'. Bert Trautmann was not a man to take banter from the young guns of Manchester City.

These players in the October of 1962 were to be the leading lights in one of Manchester City's most successful Youth Cup teams of all time.

By October 1963 most of the above players had Central league experience with a few having made their debut in the First Team.

Glyn Pardoe was a regular in the First Team squad. However nobody at the time thought anything about a cup run, we were just concentrating on being selected, winning our first game at Maine Road and holding our place in the team.

I found myself selected to play at centre forward with Glyn in the old fashioned inside right position. To find myself playing alongside and English Schools Centre Forward and First Team player left me in awe.

The opening game against Oldham Athletic was on Monday 18th November the day before my Birthday and what a present it was.

Under the floodlights at Maine Road, winning 4-1, scoring and having 'assists' in the other three goals. The adrenalin was flowing from all the players on that night and the goal I scored settled my nerves. Glyn Pardoe was not only a very good player but also an excellent team player. I learned a lot in those first games with Glyn and we became an effective partnership, scoring goals in our first games together.

All the Youth team cup games were under floodlights and I always seemed to raise my game for these matches. Turning out under the lights at Maine Road was and still is one of the biggest thrills of my football career. Anybody who loves and supports Manchester City must dream of pulling on the light blue shirt and running out under the lights at Maine Road (or The Etihad nowadays) to play for our great club.

I realised this dream and to this day I feel privileged to have had the opportunity to do this.

The Youth cup run is well chronicled in Colin Schindlers excellent book "George Best and 21 others", but it would be remiss of me to go past this exciting period of my career without telling my own story of this time again.

MANCHESTER CITY

Concilio et Labore
Wisdom and Effort

Manchester City Football Club had been born on 1ˢᵗ September 1894 and was known as Ardwick. They played their first game against local rivals Bury. Prior to this they had various name changes and ground changes.

First formed in 1880 as St Marks in West Gorton, a football team was established. Its home ground was initially in Clowes Street (the legendary Billy Meredith was married at St Mark's Anglican Church and lived on Clowes Street) before the team moved to Kirkmanshulme Cricket Club on Redgate Lane, Gorton.

The first registered game was in 1880 with West Gorton losing to Macclesfield Baptist Church 2-1. West Gorton won their first game against Stalybridge Clarence on the last day of the 1880/81 season.

They amalgamated with Gorton Athletic in 1883/84 which didn't last long and they moved to Pink Bank Lane and simplifying their name to Gorton FC.

The Church Warden, a Mr Beastow, donated a new strip to the team – a striking all-black jersey with a silver Maltese cross on the front (significant for me as my wife Therese is Maltese). The Church Warden may have had some links to the Knights Hospitallers who originated from the Knights who were given Malta by Charles 1 of Spain in 1530. The Christian based St John Ambulance Brigade formed in 1877 in the United Kingdom and was obviously impressed with the emblem.

Another ground move to Reddish Lane followed before land was acquired on Hyde Road in 1887.

As the Club had stepped out of the Gorton boundaries with this acquisition they re-named themselves as Ardwick FC after their new home town.

A local brewer, Stephen Thompson, who later became President of Ardwick FC, paid for the re-turfing of the ground and with the help of local builders constructed a stand and aided with other vital improvements.

As the 1888/89 season arrived the Manchester football season was burgeoning with the evolvement of Heaton Park, Gorton Villa and Newton Heath (later to become Manchester United).

Along with Ardwick, these teams were raising their local profiles. Ardwick at this stage made the first significant step by signing on its first professional player, Jack Hodges, who earned five shillings a week (25p in new money).

This caused consternation amongst his team mates who struggled to get expenses, and strike action was threatened.

Where have I heard that before? York City in 1973 and Rochdale in 1980 both come to mind.

Hooliganism, as mentioned previously, was recorded in the reign of Edward II in 1347 and again it reared its ugly head in February 1889 when a game between Lower Hurst and Ardwick was abandoned because of a crowd invasion (Manchester United and Manchester City comes to mind when United were relegated in 1974).

Later that same season a match against West Manchester was abandoned because two players were fighting.

In December 1891 the unthinkable occurred when an unnamed Ardwick player who was being barracked by a member of the crowd, disillusioned with a 4-0 hammering by Sheffield Wednesday, lashed out at the barracker. According to the records, the player vaulted the fence and "severely battered said spectator".

Two incidents from more recent days come to mind: Bill Leivers for Manchester City at West Bromwich Albion in 1964 when Bill had enough of a barracker and kicked the ball into the stand near the perpetrator and followed it over the wall and came back with a grim smile on his face. No more barracking, and I don't remember seeing said spectator after that.

Also everybody will be aware of the Eric Cantona episode at Crystal Palace in 1995. Sent off in the second half he stated that he was verbally abused by a Palace fan so he jumped into the crowd and Kung-Fu'd him. Cantona got a lengthy ban and a £20,000 fine for his troubles.

Ardwick prospered on the field at Hyde Road, gaining a substantial fan base with regular crowds of over 5,000.

In 1889 the Football Combination (a league of clubs who failed to get into the Football League) was disbanded and the Football Alliance was founded as a replacement. Ardwick joined the Alliance in 1891/92 season together with teams such as Nottingham Forest, Newton Heath, Sheffield Wednesday, Crewe Alexandra and Small Heath (later to become Birmingham City)

The Club was invited into the Football League in 1892 in the Second Division and there first game of the season saw them beat Bootle 7-0.

However the following years were difficult for the Ardwick Club with financial problems and they had to apply for re-election in 1893/94.

The necessity for change and the need for upheaval meant the days of Ardwick Football Club were numbered.

They became a Limited Company and changed the name to Manchester City.

From the brink of disaster a revitalised and rejuvenated Club rose from the ashes and in the space of 30 years had secured promotion to Division One and won the Cup in 1904.

However just as Manchester City were looking to emerge as England's top side in 1904 it was revealed that the club had been involved in financial irregularities which included paying £6 or £7 a week when the National wage limit was £4 per week. The authorities were furious with the Club and dismissed five of the directors and banning four players from ever turning out for the Club again.

City then played at Hyde Road until 1922 and moved to Maine Road, my spiritual home, for the 1923 season.

Moss Side was the designated area and land was bought off Jackson's brick works. Maine Road took three years to construct and was the envy of the Football League.

Manchester City played their first game at Maine Road in front of 60,000 fans in August 1923. City beat Sheffield United 2-0 with goals from Horace Barnes and Tommy Johnson. Captain on that day was Max Woosnam, little known by many today but a multi-talented sportsman. He played cricket for England, won a tennis doubles medal at Wimbledon and an Olympic gold for tennis as well; beat that, Andy Murray!

Nostalgically Maine Road was the spiritual home for me and millions of City' supporters through the years until they moved to the City of Manchester Stadium in 2003 (now the Etihad).

And now I was one of the privileged footballers to be playing there too.

A FOOTBALL ODYSSEY –
MANCHESTER CITY 1963/1964

Superbia in proello
Pride in Battle

Thinking of the Youth teams of Manchester City and Manchester United at that time, some may say who and why and what is the story worth telling? But this was the era of George Best, David Sadler John Aston and Willie Anderson at Manchester United and Glyn Pardoe, Mike Doyle, Dave Connor (and me!) at Manchester City. Suddenly you look at the photos of that era and names flood back and during that year of 1963/64 the two Manchester giants were on a collision course to meet in a Youth Cup final.

To see why this collision was so important you have to look into the state of the clubs at that time.

Manchester City were in Division Two and Manchester United had just avoided relegation a year earlier. The sides would not meet in a Derby game for a couple of seasons, so the prospect of the young hopefuls of City and United meeting had fired the imagination of the whole of Manchester.

My own concern in those days was getting into the Manchester City Youth team and attempting to hold a place down in the Central League side.

Looking back I now realise how privileged I was to pull on the light blue number 9 shirt at Maine Road and also be in the same team as Manchester City's legendary goalkeeper Bert Trautmann.

Bert was in the Lutwaffe as a radio operator but transferred to Spandau where he became a a paratrooper and served on the Eastern Front in 1941. His medals from Germany included the Iron Cross

First Class. He was in France in 1944 when the allies invaded and had to flee to avoid capture and head back to Bremen. He was caught by the Americans and interrogated and then thought he was going to be shot so escaped, then jumped a hedge and landed luckily in the hands of the British. Bert was imprisoned near Ostend in Belgium where my Uncle's regiment the Signals were stationed, though they did not meet at that time.

Bert was classified as a category "C" prisoner by the authorities meaning he was regarded as a Nazi, and after interrogation was sent to a prisoner of war camp at Marbury Hall, near Northwich, Cheshire. When he was downgraded to a Non-Nazi "B" prisoner he went to PoW Camp 50 (now Byrchall High School) in Ashton-in-Makerfield in Lancashire where he stayed until 1948. When the camps were going to be shut and repatriation was imminent, Bert chose to stay in England working first on a farm in Milnthorpe and then on bomb disposal in Huyton.

He played for St Helens Town in the Football Combination in 1948-49 and was brilliant for them and it was no surprise that the Football League clubs took an interest. In October 1949 Bert signed for Manchester City and became the first player to wear Adidas thanks to his friendship with their founder, Adolf Dassler.

It wasn't smooth sailing for Bert, being a German paratrooper replacing the legendary Frank Swift in goal. He was aided by Eric Westwood the Manchester City captain who was a Normandy veteran who made a public display of welcoming Bert, saying, "There's no war in the dressing room". Bert made his debut on my fourth birthday, 19th November 1949 and against the Club I was to support as a lad, Bolton Wanderers.

Alan Ogley, who was to become our goalkeeper in the Youth team always said that one of his boyhood heroes was Bert and he was his main reason for signing for Manchester City.

Alan signed for Manchester City as a professional from Barnsley in 1963 as an understudy to Harry Dowd (although Bert was still on the books and playing for the Club). It wasn't really a good time for Alan to be going to Maine Road as they had just drawn 1-1 with

Manchester United in the last home match of the season and were destined to relegation to Division Two.

Bert was an excellent shot-stopper, as was Alan and both had a good percentage rate on penalties saved. Neil Young used to say that the only way to beat Bert was to mis-hit your shot as he could somehow read your thoughts and the corner you were going to try and score in.

Matt Busby went so far as to say: "Don't think about the penalty, just run up and hit it and think afterwards."

Bert was a great goalkeeper even at the end of his career, a real gentleman and an inspiring figure for a young aspiring footballer like me. However he was as a man who had come through the horrors of war and an ex-paratrooper – not a man to joke with.

It is hard to believe that I was still an amateur player living on 50 shillings expenses and not knowing if I had any sort of career in professional football at this time. I was still at school when the 1963-1964 Football League season started but found myself playing in the Lancashire League Division A side after a few weeks.

Most of the Lancashire League games were played at the training grounds like The Cliff (Manchester United), Squires Gate (Blackpool) and Bellfield (where Everton trained and played).

However Rochdale Reserves played at Spotland and this gave me my first opportunity of playing on a Football League Ground.

Rochdale played a significant part in my career but this was going to be my first game at Spotland. I scored two goals in a 2-2 draw which led me onto a run of games in what was equivalent to the third team.

Another five goals in five appearances must have caught the eye of the management (I am sure Dick Neilson along with Jonny Hart and Harry Godwin had something to do with it) and I found myself being selected for the Central League side against Bolton Wanderers at Maine Road.

A dream come true: I was still at Grammar school and I was going to step onto Maine Road as a player for the first time. I will always remember that game. I was playing against one of my boyhood heroes Centre Half Bryan Edwards of Bolton Wanderers. The score was 1-1 and I got the goal, a left wing corner which I glanced in with my head. The ungracious Mike Doyle who was also playing said it hit me on the shoulder but who cared? Chalk one up to Jones!

Also in the team on that day were Bobby Kennedy, Alf Wood and Paul Aimson, who York fans would know as one of their best ever centre forwards.

Paul was born in Macclesfield in 1943 and joined Manchester City as a junior and signed professional forms in 1960. He made a number of appearances for City before he was transferred to York City for £1,000 in 1964. On 14th March 1964 I was still an amateur but had the privilege of playing at Maine Road in a reserve game, against Newcastle United, with Bert Trautmann, David Wagstaffe (sadly passed away) Bill Leivers, Alf Wood, David Shawcross and of course Paul.

York gained promotion in his first year before he was transferred to Bury for £10,000. After spells at Bradford City and Huddersfield he was transferred to York again for £8,000 in August 1969. He was part of the York City promotion side of 1970-71 and at York scored 98 goals before leaving for Bournemouth in March 1973.

I was Paul's replacement at York in June 1973 and even moved with my wife Therese into the house in Moorcroft Road that Paul had vacated.

Sadly, Paul, like Mike Doyle and David Wagstaffe, has passed away but every player I mention in this book had great footballing ability and would stand the test of time in the modern game.

Throughout the remainder of 1963 I was in and out of the Central League side but I was pleased to find that I was selected for Manchester City in the FA Youth Cup against Oldham Athletic in November of 1963.

We won the game 4-1 and I scored a couple of goals under the lights at a very wet (wasn't it always?) Maine Road. It was a great thrill and I can remember the goals to this day – one with either foot from 12 yards at the Platt Lane end.

Burnley were next up and I was still in the team and linking up very well with Glyn Pardoe and that game was also to be played under the lights at Maine Road.

We won 4-1 and I scored. Glyn, the most experienced of our Youth team players, was great to play with and helped my development tremendously.

Suddenly the young blue half of Manchester was starting to excite City supporters. Deprived of the opportunity to watch a derby match, the footballing City of Manchester suddenly realised that there was an abundance of talent on view at Youth level and speculation was rife on which team, City or United would come out on top if they met.

I held my place in the Youth team and we went on to beat Preston North End 3-1 at Preston in a second replay in the third round.

The first match had been a 0-0 draw at Maine Road. The replay was abandoned in extra time when the whole ground at Deepdale was enveloped in fog. We were losing 3-1 at the time and Howard Kendall, their star player, was running riot in midfield, creating chance after chance for his team mates. It was a strange night as the fog descended for about half an hour and the game was called off by the referee. As soon as we left the ground it cleared up and I thought: *fate was on our side.*

It got even better as Howard Kendall had been called up for the first team (later to be the youngest player to play in a Wembley Cup Final) and was missing when we went back to Deepdale the following week. We were right on our game that night and without Howard Kendall in their ranks Preston were struggling to find any rhythm. We took advantage and a couple of goals from me and another from Glyn saw us through to the next round.

We went on to beat Middlesborough who had in their ranks Arthur Horsfield who would become a team mate of mine at Swindon Town. We were really starting to play well as a team and probably turned in our best performance so far. I had a perfect milestone in the game by scoring a hat-trick. Playing at Maine Road was always a great thrill, scoring at Maine Road was even better, but to actually score a hat-trick on that hallowed turf was what dreams are made of.

This prompted the quote from George Poyser, the Manager, that I was worth £15,000 of any club's money. I chuckled over that as "any club" could have put in seven days' written notice to City and picked me up for nothing as I was still an amateur.

However I only had my sights on staying in the Central League team, scoring goals (it is the greatest thrill in football to see the ball hit the back of the net), always with one eye on the neighbours at Old Trafford. They, of course, were still winning in the Youth Cup, some of the players already having made their debuts for the United firsts ; and of course the mercurial George Best was in the background waiting to come on to centre stage.

The fifth round of the Youth Cup was to be our biggest test, over the Pennines to play Leeds United at Elland Road.

In the Leeds ranks were David Harvey, Rod Belfitt, Terry Hibbitt, Jimmy Greenhoff and two players I got to know very well later when playing for Leeds United Former Players – PeterLorimer and Eddy Gray. The great John Charles also became a good friend and it was a privilege to know these players in later years.

This was a close encounter and we came out winners 4-3 and I was pleased to have got a couple including the winner.

After the game it was rumoured Don Revie wanted to talk to me about the winner which I may have controlled with my hand before shooting us into the semi-final and our date with destiny: Manchester United.

This was to be a two-legged affair with the first leg at Old Trafford and the second leg back at Maine Road.

Back in leafy Altrincham it was hard to believe that a few miles up the road to Moss Side and a few miles up the other road to Stretford, Manchester was in a fever of excitement about the two Youth sides meeting. Some of us had only just started shaving – we were that young – and yet the blue half of Manchester expected us to hold up the honour of the City and beat the old enemy.

The first leg of the Youth team derby attracted 29,706 fans at Old Trafford and caught the imagination of United and City fans alike. It is still unbelievable to me even now that over 50,000 fans watched the two legs. In comparison, when Manchester United played their home leg of the semi-final in 1962 only 4,000 fans turned up at Old Trafford.

George Best, who had not made an appearance for the Youth team, and who was playing regularly in Manchester United's first team, was selected for these games, a tribute, we considered, to our half of

Manchester: we were not to be taken lightly. George had also been selected for his first International for Northern Ireland and even that did not stop his appearance in what was seen as a bigger challenge.

Mike Doyle, who had a malevolent dislike of anything red, especially United, stoked up the game but it failed to live up to its billing as a spectacle.

His enmity for United would last throughout his career and it was the well documented feud with George Best that may indirectly have led to my mate Glyn Pardoe getting his leg broken in a tackle with George Best in the derby in December 1970. Mike scored at the Stretford end and then something may have been said between him and George. Then came the slide tackle with six studs showing that gave Glyn a double fracture. Only George knew whether it was meant as a leg-breaker, or just a mis-timed tackle. Knowing the players I think that George lost control of the ball and just followed it in frustration and was late. Glyn was too quick and as both players had courage they never shirked the collision with a horrible result.

Glyn was to be out of the game for two years and never really got back to his old form, but we did meet up again in the two games between York City and Manchester City in the League Cup in 1973.

But back to 1963/4: United won the first leg of the Youth Cup semi-final 4-1 but it became a game of flying tackles, nasty fouls, only lifted by some class play from John Aston who eclipsed George Best and put us to the sword. The bragging rights were firmly in United's court.

However there was the little matter of the second leg a fortnight later and we players in the light blue, disappointed though we were, intended to show our half of Manchester the reason why we had reached the semi-final.

Between games I had found out that the apprentices in the team had been offered contracts and as nobody had said anything to me about the future I was quite concerned; I wondered if the 4-1 defeat at Old Trafford had scuppered my ambitions. It looked like I had to again pluck up courage and ask about my future.

This became very difficult as it was the week when all of Manchester was looking forward to Bert Trautmann's testimonial match at Maine

Road. This was a game which attracted one of the largest attendances for such a game. If you look at the records it says the official attendance was 47,951 but I was there and the whole of Maine Road was packed and a more realistic figure would be 60,000. It was to be a memorable night not just for Bert, but for me as well.

It was Wednesday 15th April 1964, and a Manchester XI played an England XI. The Manchester side included Denis Law, Bobby Charlton and Derek Kevan and, of course, Bert, while England had Stanley Matthews, Tom Finney, Ronnie Clayton and Jimmy Armfield in the line–up.

The records say that Manchester won 5-4 but the game was finally ended by the fans who swept on to the pitch to say farewell to Bert Trautmann.

I remember it for other reasons. I followed the players down the tunnel at the end of the game, once they had fought their way through the fans in front of the main stand. Ahead of me off to one side near the gymnasium were George Poyser and Harry Godwin. I do not know why I picked that moment but they looked aside from the jubilant celebrations down on the pitch. So I said, "Boss, could I have a quick word with you?" Harry Godwin, bless him, must have anticipated what I was going to ask and he said, "Chris, we had just been discussing you, and we are going to offer you a professional contract."

The jubilation of the crowd could not match my excitement at those few words and I will be for ever grateful to Harry Godwin, not only picking me out at the trial at Urmston two years earlier, but for putting me out of my misery on that night and affirming I had a future at Manchester City.

Excitement and elation and the emotion of the moment overtook me outside the ground and I was crying and laughing as the fans drifted away from Maine Road.

How could I let my Uncle Bill know as quickly as possible? No mobiles to text or phone and the telephone box in Platt Lane, Moss Side was always vandalised and out of order. At that moment I could have run it home just like Pheidippides striding out with the good news from Marathon to Athens in 490 BC. However it was back to the mundane way I always travelled to Altrincham, catching the bus with the stragglers from the match to Oxford Road in Manchester and then the electric train to Altrincham. I was bursting with the good news by then and every stop seemed an eternity – Stretford, Sale, Brooklands, Timperley and Navigation Road, before arriving in Altrincham. Then it was a race up the ramp and over Moss Lane Bridge to arrive home in Hamon Road with the good news.

As always my Uncle Bill took it phlegmatically and just smiled as if to say: *I always knew you had the determination and ability to make it.* I looked back and thought, *but not without you I couldn't have done it.* Aunt Hazel always took a practical view on the situation and asked if I would like some *Naked City* stew? This was a stew in a dark gravy with chump chops, dumplings, potatoes and carrots and was always on the gas. I always seemed to arrive back from training about the time the American cult series *Naked City* was on our black and white 14-inch TV – hence the name of the stew.

The show, about the NYPD, ran in an hour-long format from 1960-63 and always finished with the words, *There are eight million stories in the Naked City. This has been one of them.* Well, on this night the only story worth telling was of my signing for Manchester City – but the stew was still very good. It was a great night of excitement in our household, although tempered with the knowledge that the hard work of playing and retaining my position as a professional was to come and that the game was going to throw up many trials and tribulations along the way as well as its moments of glory and excitement.

Bill also reminded me that I had training the following morning and maybe a Central League game on the Saturday before the big return leg in the Youth Cup against Manchester United on the following Monday.

Phil Burrows, Ron Frost, John Clay, Mike Doyle and me were all signed as professionals by the Club on the same day in May 1964. Only three amateurs were signed professional from the original group of trialists back in 1962. Geoff Howard, who didn't play in the semi-finals, was released.

They didn't take us lightly: again George Best was in the line-up even though his first International appearance was due against Wales at Swansea the following Saturday. Looking back, George played eight competitive league, cup and international games in 16 days including the Youth Cup semi-finals. Can you imagine players and managers today allowing this? But players would rather play than train and there is too much talk of burn-out today. If you love the game you play as often as you can for as long as you can.

The return leg was a much closer affair although we were always playing catch-up. It was a grim, wet and murky night at Maine Road but at least the teams played to the quality, skill and standards expected of two great Clubs that had reached the semi-final of the Youth Cup.

Manchester United scored first but Glyn Pardoe soon equalised. In the second half we exchanged goals: George Best got one and David Sadler a couple, including the winner, and Glyn and Bobby McAlinden scored for us. We came out of the game with our heads held high even though it was a bitter pill to swallow losing 4-3 in the last minute.

Another great crowd of over 20,000 fans saw the game and when you consider that Manchester City's home gate that season averaged 15,000 supporters it was a great tribute to the young sides. Overall the two games were watched by over 50,000 fans and both United and City considered the future of the Manchester sides to be in the capable hands of the current crop of young players on show that night.

Manchester went on to demolish Don Rogers and his Swindon Town team in the two-legged final. Drawing at the County Ground where Don Rogers scored (later to be a team mate when I was transferred to Swindon), they won 4-1 at Old Trafford with a good friend of mine David Sadler getting a hat-trick.

However all of Manchester saw the City-United game as the real final in 1964. The game is still talked about and books are still written about of the Manchester young guns of 1963/1964.

For my part it was a privilege to have been part of what was a memorable time for the two Manchester Clubs at Youth level and at a time when the senior teams were going through transitional periods.

But I still have nightmares about two good chances to score at Old Trafford that April night when I did not convert either one. My tally for that Youth Cup run was ten goals, and to this day it sticks in my craw that I did not score against the old enemy.

The teams for those epic semi-finals in April of 1964 were: Manchester City: Alan Ogley, David Wild, Mike Doyle, Alf Wood, Phil Burrows, John Clay, Bobby McAlinden, Dave Connor, Max Brown (Ron Frost), Glyn Pardoe, Chris Jones.

Manchester United: Jimmy Rimmer, Alan Duff, David Farrar, Peter McBride, Bobby Noble, John Fitzpatrick, Albert Kinsey, Willie Anderson, David Sadler, George Best, John Aston.

At the end of the season the lads who had been offered professional contracts were elated. We were only on £12 a week but that did not matter as we considered ourselves to be privileged to be Manchester City players and to do what we always wanted to do and that was to have the opportunity to play football at the highest level possible. I still have kept my first pay packet from Walter Griffith, the Secretary, which shows £12 and a signing-on fee of £20 as well as a telegram asking me to report for pre-season training at Maine Road.

However that was a few steps away and Manchester City had the problem of getting out of the Second Division.

While we were reaching the Youth Cup semi-final the first team had only finished sixth in the Second Division (now the Championship) even though they had two prolific goal scorers in Jimmy Murray and Derek Kevan.

I learned a lot from Jimmy Murray who had been a quality striker at Wolves and during the 1965/1966 season would get to play quite a few games with him in the Central League side. Holding the ball up, making diagonal runs and creating space for team mates to go into all came from working with Jimmy Murray, a true professional who sadly passed away a few years ago.

THE PROFESSIONAL YEARS AT
MANCHESTER CITY 1964-1965

I signed the professional forms for Manchester City in May of 1964 in front of George Poyser the Manager, Walter Griffith the Secretary and the man who picked me out two years before – Harry Godwin, the Chief Scout.

In those days it was a year's contract with an option for the club to take you on for a second year. The football clubs at this time still had all the power and all the players were like indentured serfs until 1961 when the maximum wage was abolished.

The retained and transfer system still kept the players at the mercy of the clubs, no matter what the weekly wage we were on. Many has been the time when April arrived and the two lists were put on the notice board to say whether you had a contract for the following year or were collecting your cards to go looking for another club.

I always found that to be a disheartening moment, seeing good players turning disconsolately away knowing their time at the club had ended. I vowed this would not happen to me if I could help it.

It wasn't until 1963 that Mr Justice Wilberforce declared the system illegal after Jimmy Hill of the Professional Footballers' Association and Newcastle United had fought a lengthy and costly legal action over the transfer of George Eastham to Arsenal.

This was a long time before agents did the negotiating for a player and I was glad at just putting pen to paper and looking forward to the pre-season which started for us in late June.

During the close-season some of the younger players liked to go into Maine Road for a game of skittle-ball or head tennis.. Usually it involved Jonny Hart and Dave Ewing (didn't they have homes to go to)? That always meant a hard morning as they didn't like to lose.

If players like Dave Connor and myself got on a winning streak against them we knew we were in for a long day as we never got out of Maine Road until they had thrashed us. We must have been masochistic as Dave and I always went back for more.

George Poyser had managed Notts County from 1953-1957 before he joined Manchester City as Assistant with his main duties as Chief Scout.

In 1963 Les Mcdowall left the Club and George took over as Manager with Harry Godwin taking over as Chief Scout. George made three big signings for City in Derek Kevan, Johnny Crossan and Jimmy Murray. He also promoted home grown talent in Alan Oakes and Glyn Pardoe who formed my striking partnership in the Youth team. Jimmy Murray was part of the side that won promotion to the First Division in 1965-66 and along with Derek Kevan were prolific goal scorers for the Club.

As a young player I wondered how I could get anywhere near the levels these two strikers were reaching and felt slightly disheartened. However I had Dick Neilson, Johnny Hart and Harry Godwin to keep my spirits up and always had that determined stubborn streak which said "keep going".

My first year was one of Lancashire League games and finally cementing a position as a professional in the Central League side.

As I was training with the likes of Kevan, Murray and Crossan along with many experienced professionals, the summit of the first team in that first year did not seem so far away.

I had 15 goals in 20 appearances for the Central League side by February 1965 and thought I was moving in the right direction.

The second season for George Poyser was becoming a bit of a nightmare and the month before the Club had just had its lowest attendance figure at Maine Road for a League game, 8,015 against Swindon Town. The writing was on the wall for the Manager and the Club, and as I saw it as a young player, needed an overhaul and a fresh approach. It needed a spring- clean and probably a reduction in playing staff as it always seemed we had professionals on the sidelines or playing in the Lancashire League A team. I hoped if this happened the goals I was scoring in the Central League would mean the Club would exercise the option on my contract and keep me on.

Then disaster struck for me at Maine Road on the 13th March 1965 against Everton Reserves. Opposing me was George Heslop of Everton, soon to become a Manchester City player. Tackles from behind was a hazard a centre forward had to live with in those days as centre halves used to lick their lips when seeing a young cocky centre forward learning the ropes. John Clay, who along with Phil Burrows, had graduated into the Central League team, played the ball into me. I held it up and was just about to lay it off when "wham"! A boot swiped right through me and the ball and smashed into the outside of my right leg. Down I went and on came Dave Ewing with the magic sponge (freezing cold water).

I was hurt this time I knew, but, daft like, got up. Dave said, "Are you all right kid?" and so as not to let Heslop know he had nailed me I said, "OK Dave, I will try and run it off." He helped me to my feet and I hobbled around as the game carried on. I knew something was wrong with my leg but John Hart had always told me and Dave Connor not to let the opposition know they had hurt you – get up and play on. Somehow I carried on round the periphery of the game before John Clay passed the ball into my feet and as I controlled it my leg gave way. Dave rushed on this time and carried me off like a babe in arms. I had somehow survived ten minutes with what I thought was a badly bruised leg.

The game ended and the Club paid for a taxi back to Altrincham I was told to ice the leg and report for treatment on Monday morning. I couldn't move for the rest of the weekend and phoned Glyn Pardoe for a lift on the Monday. He and Alan Oakes sometimes came through Altrincham from Winsford and they agreed to pick me up at Altrincham crossing. I had to hobble three quarters of a mile from my house in Hamon Road and with the help of my old Gran's walking sticks made it to the crossing, beads of sweat pouring down my face and knowing my leg was not right.

The "country cousins" (they lived out in the Cheshire countryside) thought it was a great laugh seeing me with these two walking sticks but I was in agony and didn't see the funny side. Alan then said you had better have a word with the Club and get an X-ray on that leg. Only then did it flash across my mind that it might be broken.

Johnny Hart came into the dressing room and said I was to go with David Shawcross, another injured player, to see the specialist in the City centre and have an X-ray. The result was that Shawky had just a sprain. In my case the specialist told me to stay where I was as I had a broken fibula and not to attempt any weight on it. He said he had notified the Club and a taxi was arranged to take me up to the Manchester Royal Infirmary and get the leg put in plaster.

I was mortified: my season was over and the question of my future career at Manchester City in abeyance as the Club floundered and the night of the long knives could happen and many players swept out of the Club in a savage purge.

Out of action and out of sight I could only watch from home as George Poyser was sacked and the team finish a disappointing 11th in the League. I sat doing jig-saws and once a week went by ambulance up to the Manchester Royal Infirmary, fretting my time away worrying about my future. Finally I was allowed to travel to and from the ground and the Club paid for the taxis.

The first men I saw as I arrived on crutches were Johnny and Harry. I said, like I did 12 months before, "What's going to happen to me, John?" His reply was, "Keep your head down and you will be here next season." I was relieved and said, "Thanks, John.". Only now when I reminisce about that time do I think that a new broom might have swept clean and even the likes of Johnny, Dave and Harry might have been victims. However, I think they knew who might be the new Manager and also the way the Board were thinking.

I was expected to be in plaster for three weeks but they took it off and then replaced it with a lighter one for another three weeks. By then I had received a telegram from Walter Griffith stating that I had been retained, which took a great weight off my mind as my dream of reaching the first team was still alive.

The new Manager was Joe Mercer who arrived in the middle of July 1965.

BLUE MOON RISING 1965-1966

In principio Allison anno Mercer.
The start of the Mercer-Allison years at Manchester City.

Within a month, Joe Mercer, who had been ill and suffered a stroke at Aston Villa and had been fired, decided he needed an Assistant and Malcolm Allison was his choice.

Mal had originally played for Charlton Athletic but he told the bosses what he thought about the stagnating fitness and training methods and left. In 1951 he ended up at West Ham United which was ideal for Malcolm where as a great thinker about the game, tactics and skills were listened to and acted on.

In 1957 Malcolm's playing career as a centre back came to an end when he contracted tuberculosis and had to have a lung removed. He drifted out of the game but then joined the West Ham coaching staff under Ted Fenton and became a leading innovator in the establishment of the academy principles.

Malcolm always told us about mentoring the young Bobby Moore and related to him when he talked to the younger players like myself at Manchester City. Always, it was positive thinking about skills, fitness, movement aspirations and belief, and the confidence to succeed as a top player at Manchester City.

Malcolm arrived at Chassen Road and we saw him for the first time and I think most of the younger players were overawed by his entrance. Me, I was just scared to death. Here was this big man in a bright red tracksuit top not just breezing in to take training but blowing in like a hurricane. There was a quick introduction to the players and then into a very demanding but enjoyable training session with plenty of ball work.

Looking back, as a coach he was obviously looking for reactions and carefully monitoring everybody and everything that went on. Big, brash, arrogant, you may call him all these things, but he was a success man and wanted to take as many of the players on board with him as he could.

I was still feeling my way back from my broken leg but the man had already done his homework on every player on the pitch and knew who he was going to take along and those he decided were going to fall by the wayside or actually push them over the edge. Brutal was football throughout the ages and no different in the 1960s.

This was obviously what the Club needed at the time as lethargy had set in and some players were just playing for the wages and not for the traditions of a great club like Manchester City.

The only success City had during recent seasons were from the Youth team I played in, but it needed more than young players learning the game to lift City out of the doldrums. Malcolm, with Joe Mercer to rein him back, was that breath of fresh air at the time. Johnny Hart, Dave Ewing and Harry Godwin from the "old school" I was never sure how they took Mal but results came and Manchester City was their Club through thick and thin.

Malcolm changed a lot of things in the early days especially with regard to fitness training, skill factors, and style of living. The last was on the basis of the old adage do as I say, not as I do, as I was to find out to my cost at a later date.

However he liked players with flare but who could also put in the work rate as well. He had studied some teams in Germany and also as a defender knew the value of keeping clean sheets. To that end he brought in Tony Book as a right back who could also sweep across the back four. Mal called it the German Bolt (locking the door on the forward players). We were never classed as a defensive side and he always preached to us that if we had passed square, the next pass had to go forward. In the days when everybody preached that possession was nine tenths of the law, a player like Ray Wilkins of Manchester United would never have got a game. He was called the crab for playing endlessly across the pitch with the square pass whereas the

Manchester City players always looked to penetrate defences with a forward pass.

After a few years of Malcolm and Joe we had players who could perfect it in Colin Bell and Mike Summerbee, and later Francis Lee. Yes, we had to do the same in the reserve team and knew if we got our chance that the same system would still be in place if we got our chance in the first team.

YOUNG GUN SHOT DOWN

As a young professional I had a couple of Triumph Spitfires, a white one and the other, God forgive me, in RED. Why I had two cars I never knew but on this particular Wednesday night I was bored back in Altrincham and decided to take the car for a run out. It was about 8pm and I ended up at Bredbury Hall near Stockport where a lot of the "Cheshire Set" and City players used to go. I went into the Club but it was quiet so I moved on and decided to head into Manchester. At a loose end, I ended up in Whitworth Street where The Twisted Wheel was located. It was a great scene in Manchester in the 60s, with lots of well-known groups: St Louis Union, the Hollies, the American soul singer Ben E King, Kenny Lynch, The Steam Packet (with Rod Stewart, Long John Baldry, Brian Auger and Julie Driscoll) all doing cabaret.

Mixed in amongst were new stars from TV and *Coronation Street*, Mike and Bernie Winters, Sid and Eddy (who became Little and Large), Gerry Harris who ran the Piccadilly Club and of course the new sporting stars of the Manchester scene like George Best and Mike Summerbee. The Manchester scene was thriving as were the Cavern in Liverpool and the King's Road in Chelsea.

Top of the Pops had its first airing from the Dickenson Road studio in Rusholme, Manchester in 1964. With the stars like the Rolling Stones, The Hollies, Dusty Springfield and the Beatles playing the hits of the time, the cameras would pan around to bring in various celebrities including sporting stars dancing to the music. Of course George Best was one of the noted figures often televised.

The Club the City lads tended to frequent was Tiffany's in Oxford Road where the Les Nocturnes used to reside. The main singers in the group were Sandra Stevens, who became the lead singer in Brotherhood of Man, and Eve Eden who changed her name to Eve

Graham and joined the New Seekers. It was Eve's voice on the most famous commercial of all time, Coca-Cola's *I'd like to teach the world to sing*. Lynn Paul was also in the group and went on to join the New Seekers as well before having a long solo career in cabaret and television.

After the Twisted Wheel I moved onto Mr Smiths in John Ogden Street., I knew Jimmy, the bouncer on the door at Mr Smiths. I asked Jimmy if much was happening and he said, no it was a quiet night, go in and get a drink. *Bad move!* I walked down the steps and across the room was Malcolm Allison entertaining some friends, including Paul Docherty, a reporter, and Jerry Harris, a really good comedian from the Piccadilly Club. But none of my footballing mates was there.. I was mortified: a young player out mid-week and I had walked into the lion's den. I did a quick about turn, heading for the steps and I thought I had made it when a familiar voice shouted my nickname: "Jazzer, come and join us." I went over to the table and Mal asked, "Would you like some food or a Bacardi and Coke". Not falling for that one, I thought. "Just a Coke Malcolm, thank you". The group all just carried on talking as if I wasn't there and I squirmed around for about 15 minutes before I plucked up the courage to say I was going home. All Malcolm said was, "OK, see you tomorrow," and it sounded like the voice of doom descending.

It was with considerable trepidation that I arrived the following morning for training. Nothing happened. I trained as hard as I could and kept my head below the parapet that morning. Had I got away with last night's misdemeanour? It looked like it.

Back in the dressing room I was having a chat with Dave Connor about a trip into Manchester and having a look at the shops during the afternoon and maybe calling in at Tiffany's to listen to the music there.

It looked like Malcolm had forgotten about last night. No such luck! Just as Tadger and I were leaving Jonny Hart appeared at the dressing room door. "Jonesy, back here changed at two o'clock."

"What for, John," said I innocently?

"You know," said a serious John Hart, behind him the face of his co-henchman Big Dave Ewing. At that point I knew I was in deep trouble. My mate Dave Connor thought it was amusing.

The Early Years

Bill 1939 Cheshire Yeomanry

Jessie Grandmother

*George Wardle Jones (war hero on the Somme in 1915)
and Jessie Hope Jones (seated)*

War Horse – The trek to Rosh Pina, Israel
Bill (left), Lea (father on far right)

War Horse – Lea with horses

Bill on horse Stardust in Syria 1941

Brothers – Bill, Lea, Gordon in Syria after being de-horsed in 1941

Bill and Chris on the beach playing football as usual

*Stamford Lads, spot the author – Peter Leigh front row
(who got me my trial at Manchester City) second from right*

Altrincham and Sale Boys 1958 in the snow

Manchester City Youth Team

The Youth Team 1963

Back Row: Max Brown, David Wild, Alan Ogley, Phil Burrows, Mike Doyle, John Clay

Front Row: Glyn Pardoe, Chris Jones, Alf Wood, Bobby McAlinden, Dave Connor

The youth players in training 1963

*Manchester United vs Manchester City Youths semi-final
at foggy Maine Road*

*Manchester United vs Manchester City Youths – Chris Jones and
Bobby Noble (Manchester United) fight for the ball*

Manchester City Youth programme 1964

MANCHESTER UNITED YOUTH (back row, from left): Bobby Noble, Peter McBride, John Fitzpatrick, Jimmy Rimmer, David Farrar, Alan Duff; (front row) Willie Anderson, George Best, David Sadler, Albert Kinsey, John Aston

Manchester United Youth Team – George Best

Manchester City – The First Professional Year

The Manchester City squad under George Poyser 1964/65 season

Phil Burrows and Chris Jones –
first year professionals 1964

George Poyser in 1965
with City players.
Doyle, Burrows,
Connor, and Jones in
stripes (left to right)

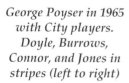

The city squad in 1966 – Chris Jones next to Jimmy Murray (top right)
John Hart (bottom right)

The Mercer Allison Years

*Joe Mercer watching
early training session*

*Chris Jones with
Mike Doyle and
Neil Young – Joe Mercer
in background*

*Dave Connor and
Chris Jones in serious pose.
Roy Cheetham thinks it's
funny*

Joe and Malcolm's squad in team formation in 1965.

Chris with his 'red' triumph spitfire - never taken to Maine Road

Chris Jones with his white triumph spitfire and boots – used this for Maine Road!

The Manchester City squad 1966/67 under Joe Mercer and Malcolm Allison

Left to right – Chris Jones, Harry Dowd,
Roy Cheetham, and Tony Coleman share a joke with legendary chief scout
Harry Godwin 1967

Johnny Hart,
Malcolm Allison and Dave
Ewing who were big influences
in Chris Jones career at
Manchester City

In civvies – (left to right)
Neil Young, Tony Book,
Chris Jones, Stan Horn,
and Harry Dowd

Debut for Manchester City – 1966/67

City call up youngster –
Roger and Chris 1966.

Chris Jones night before debut –
note the vinyls

Debut –
Nottingham Forest 1966

Chris Jones leaps over
goalkeeper
Peter Grummitt
against Nottingham Forest

Chris Jones shoots past the post

Mike Summerbee and Chris jones at Maine Road against Southampton in 1966. Drew 1-1.

Chris Jones scoring for Manchester City in 5-1 win against Bath City in December 1966.

Chris Jones and David Webb – Southampton tussling for the ball

Chris Jones and Horst Walter Eintrecht Braunshweig goal keeper challenge for the ball in Guttersloh West Germany

The Championship Year 1967/68

Manchester City at airport heading for Aberdeen in pre-season friendly

"Can I come back to watch your afternoon session as it would probably be better than going to Kendal Milne's shopping or Tiffany's?" I will not repeat my expletive response to that as Dave waved goodbye and winked at the players standing nearby.

A young cocky professional footballer I was not at the end of that day. It was 12 laps to start with, then six 60 yard sprints followed by "doggies and shuttles" (short sprints). We moved into the gym under the stands where I had to endure one-a-side skittle ball, first against Harty and then against Big Dave and anything resembling a skilful game it was not. I was hammered from pillar to post and finally crawled out to get a bath where I was physically sick.

I looked up and both John and Dave were grinning like Cheshire Cats. "That will learn you Chris," said John. Under my breath I said, "Yes, learned me not to go where Malcolm goes for his leisure moments."

THE CITY BACKROOM STAFF

However those were the days where the clubs were discreet in disciplining players and I learned a lot from such good ex-pros as Jonny Hart and Dave Ewing, along with Dick Neilson and Harry Godwin. Those four in particular I am indebted to for my footballing career. They were great men in a great time for Manchester City Football Club.

Dave Ewing was a great centre half in his day and played in two Cup Finals, one in 1955 when Manchester City lost to Newcastle United 3-1, and then on the winning side against Birmingham City in 1956 when Bert Trautmann broke his neck saving a goal. He made 279 League appearances for City but has still the unenviable record of scoring the most goals in his own net. Dave, like Paul Hince, always seemed to be there for me when I was injured: my badly cut eye at Maine Road when Ray Potter of West Bromwich Albion elbowed me, my broken leg with George Heslop against Everton and the dislocation of my left knee at Oldham. It's a wonder that I ever had time to get on the pitch and score goals, but he was always there for me and the other young players and played a large part in my development.

Dick Neilson was also a centre half and very good friends with Harty and they looked after me when I first became an amateur with Manchester City. In tough times while trying to establish myself in the B team there was always an encouraging word from Dick and maybe a tip on how to play which would stand me in good stead in future games. I am sure he always relayed my thoughts to Johnny Hart and gave a report on my improvement or otherwise. I think it was Dick who recommended me for a game in the Lancashire League A team and a game in the Manchester City Reserves while I was an amateur still at school.

Harry Godwin, Chief Scout, was thought of as the "Top Man" by young players in the 60's. He along with Johnny Hart picked me out in that trial at Chassen Road and helped to nurture me into a strong, determined footballer who could make a name in the hard game which was professional football.

Malcolm Allison was not sure of Harry when he first arrived at the Club but was soon to realise that this man was invaluable to the future success of Manchester City. An example when Malcolm first arrived was in the case of a young forward Malcolm had seen on a Sunday morning in a local league game. He rushed back to tell Harry he had a "find" and to get him watched and signed before "the other lot" got him.

"What's his name, Malcolm," asked Harry.

"Tommy Booth, get down and get him signed quick."

"No haste Malcolm, I already signed him last week."

Mal was gob-smacked and mightily impressed with this dapper little man in a trilby and after that Harry's judgment on signings was never questioned by Malcolm. Of course Tommy Booth was to become a great centre half with the Club, a good friend of mine, except when he stopped me with his nose from scoring for York City in the League Cup at Bootham Crescent in 1973.

The Saturday after my nocturnal mishap I was, of course, substitute for the Central League team and a long way, I thought, from making my debut in the first team.

Unfortunately only Johnny Hart is still alive at this moment of writing but I am indebted to John for some moments of his career which we reminisced about at the Etihad stadium at a Past Players' dinner in 2010. Manchester City had just won the Cup and the present players were parading it around the ground. John did not go out and I joined him on his table and we talked of past times. It was a real privilege to talk and we both had memories of Wembley Cup Finals missed. John missed the 1956 Cup final with a broken leg and I scored eight goals for Swindon Town but was dropped for the League Cup final against Arsenal.

It was a melancholic moment we shared, both Clubs having won without us sharing any of the glory. Carlos Tevez parading the FA Cup was just too much for us on that nostalgic evening and we stayed inside.

John told me a story of how he supplemented his income by going to a boxing booth on a Friday night and fighting. He won but broke his thumb. Manchester City was playing Bury on the Saturday but unless the goalkeeper got injured he would be OK. Sure enough, the goalkeeper went down sick just before the game and Johnny was the designated replacement and dared not tell anyone of his injury. John got away with it as he had little to do in goal.

John also told the story of how as a young player on the ground staff he would always get to Maine Road very early on a Monday morning after a home first team game. The Prestwick Brass Band played regularly at the games and they had a blanket collection for charity. Spectators used to toss the money high into the air hopefully to land in the blankets. Harty told me that on Monday mornings he used to collect more than his wages in what he found in the stands and on the track round the pitch.

When Harty told Dave Connor and me to get back in the afternoon to play head tennis and skittle ball against him and Dave Ewing it was not a punishment, or filling in the afternoon for the two trainers, but a mentoring of two young professionals.

The greatest accolade from Johnny Hart was at the Etihad at one of the dinners. He introduced me to some of his friends and said: "This is Chris Jones, he could play a bit."

From one professional to another it does not get better than that, and I was choked, filled with emotion. I never realised he rated me so much as a player until 40 years later. It was well worth waiting for, John.

MY MANCHESTER CITY DEBUT 1966-67

Mea debut in urbem Manchester

This was Manchester City's 76th season in the Football League and the first season back in the First Division. Having gained promotion in 1966 we could only manage 15th place in the Division by the close of the 1967 footballing season.

Derek Kevan had been injured half way through the season and John Crossan struggled with injuries and was finally sold to Middlesbrough.

I had been playing very well in the reserves and finished the 1965/6 season with 25 goals and was completely dismayed at being overlooked for the first team. The *Manchester Evening News* sports letter columns were full of questions why "young Jones" did not get a chance in the team while the side was struggling for goals. Even Mike Doyle had been played up front and managed to score a few. That was Malcolm's fad about height in attack and Doyley's ability in the air.

Joe defended the thinking by saying, "Jones will get his chance and is gaining the experience necessary to get into the first team". I trained really hard in the close season at Wythenshawe and our new training headquarters at Cheadle.

Joe Mercer told the press: "Jones is working hard in pre-season and has made a lot of progress, he is much sharper and is learning quickly. Jones will be in the squad to fly out to Aberdeen for a pre-season friendly."

However Ralph Brand, the Rangers and Scottish International, was also in the 14 man squad at the start of the 1966 season and I knew I had a fight on my hands to oust him from the team.

Well, I got half a game at Aberdeen in place of Ralph Brand and I suddenly realised he was not liked by Malcolm and the feeling was mutual.

There was only one winner when it came to who played for Manchester City and who was shown the door. We lost the pre-season game at Pittodrie 2-1 but considered I had put in a better performance than Ralph Brand.

We flew back to Manchester and a couple of days later were playing one of my clubs-to-be in the second pre-season friendly at Walsall. I started the game at Walsall and we were one goal up from Johnny Crossan at Fellows Park and I was feeling confident that I had shaken off Ralph Brand's challenge for a starting berth in the first team against Southampton at the Dell on the first day of the season.

But I went over on my ankle and with medial ligament damage I was to miss the start of the season. My hope of a first team start had been put on hold. City drew against Southampton 1-1 and then won their next two home games against Liverpool and Sunderland and as I recuperated I again felt I was the forgotten man in Joe and Malcolm's plans.

Goal scoring became a problem for City from the end of August, 1966 and they lost seven out of the next nine games to mid-October. Meanwhile I was back in action for the reserves and had scored 11 goals in 15 games and the papers were asking the question again: why isn't Chris Jones given a chance? City were also linked with various big-money signings for the position at the time and all I could do was work hard in training and keep sticking the ball in the net for the reserves. Joe was talking to me at the time about keeping my head up as my chance would come. But soon after he had discussed this with me the team started to win again and skuppered what I thought was my imminent debut for Manchester City.

They managed to beat Burnley, Stoke and Everton during November 1966 but not with any conviction and on the 26th November 1966 City got thrashed at Fulham 4-1. I was still scoring in the reserves and the press was clamouring for me to be given a chance as no big signing had been made. I thought to myself, "If I don't get picked now then I might as well look for another club." I had done everything physically and mentally possible to get selected".

My prayers were answered when Joe and Malcolm had me in the Manager's office and told me that I would make my debut against Nottingham Forest on the Saturday at Maine Road.

It was a huge moment in my life after a long journey from Chassen Road so many years ago. It had seemed to take an eternity but it was up to me now. Johnny Hart had said a few seasons earlier, "Chris you will have to prove your critics wrong."

I said, "What critics John"?

He replied: "Everybody has critics in this game, Chris, and the higher up you go the more critics you will have on your back. It's how you deal with them that will determine if you have a future in the game." Well, there wasn't going to be a much bigger moment than this, in front of a Manchester City crowd who were demanding we competed with the other lot across the City and started to win something.

The Manchester City team for that game had Alan Ogley in goal, Tony Book and Glyn Pardoe as full-backs, Stan Horne, Bobby Kennedy and George Heslop at the back, Johnny Crossan, Colin Bell and Dave Connor in midfield and Neil Young and myself in attack. Mike Doyle was substitute.

I had the very experienced Bob McKinlay against me at centre half who had 500 league appearances under his belt. They had Peter Grummit in goal and a potent attacking force of Joe Baker and Frank Wignall up front. Barry Lyons, who was to become one of my main providers for the goals I scored for York City, was on the right wing. Barry had just been signed from Rotherham and had made 144 league and cup appearances for them. He had scored on his debut for Forest against Sunderland three weeks earlier in a 3-1 win.

Unfortunately I did not manage to emulate Barry by scoring on my debut. In front of a 35,000 crowd at Maine Road, Forest took the lead in the 41st minute when Joe Baker side-footed the ball home. But Bobby Kennedy equalised two minutes later with a tremendous shot from outside the box, which gave Peter Grummit no chance.

I led the line well in my first game but we could not get that vital second goal in the second half. Peter Grummit was in top form in the Forest goal and when I got an opportunity when I pivoted just outside the penalty box and smashed a shot to the top right hand corner of the net. Grummit somehow managed to claw the shot away. The game ended 1-1 and the press were complimentary to my performance saying I controlled the line very well and showed glimpses of class. I came off and was given some quiet words of encouragement by Joe Mercer and Malcolm Allison and went home with some satisfaction. But had I done enough to hold my place in the team for the following game at West Bromwich Albion?

On the Monday we travelled down to play Southern league side Bath City in a testimonial match for Ron Walker at Twerton Park. Both Malcolm Allison and Tony Book had associations with Bath. We came away with a 5-1 win and having scored two goals in the match (one a 30 yard screamer), I thought I had done well.

The following Saturday we went to West Bromwich Albion and I was still in the team so had obviously done enough to please Joe and Malcolm. Alan Oakes was to come back in the team for the game and Mike Summerbee who had been out of the side with a two-week suspension was due back the following week. It was up to me to put in a performance which would give the management team something to ponder. My performance that day was to be my best for Manchester City. We had lost earlier in the season to West Bromwich Albion in the Cup and knew we were in for a tough game. The best way of describing the events of that day is to use the summarising from Peter Gardner who was the sports reporter on all City's games at the time and Gerry Harrison's notes in the City programme the following week.

It was classed as a Blues super-show and the most convincing win of the season, setting Joe Mercer the problem of who to leave out the following week when Mike Summerbee's suspension was over. I was "Monday's Man" in the *Manchester Evening News* which is hard to achieve when you are challenged by the players of United like Bobby Charlton and George Best, and all the other Lancashire Division players. I enjoyed the accolade.

Quote from Peter Gardner in the *Manchester Evening News*: *From goalkeeper Alan Ogley to outside left Neil Young there was a superb balance of defensive stability and attacking mobility.* Alan Ogley, who played in goal for the Youth team, said it was the tightest defence he had ever played behind and that George Heslop, Glyn Pardoe and his cousin Alan Oakes were the best defenders on the park. Stan Horne had done a great job marking Clive Clarke and cutting off supply to Astle and Brown while Johnny Crossan controlled the middle of the field and had an inspired match.

We won the game 3-0 and Gerry Harrison who wrote in the City programme at the time that a new problem had suddenly popped up at Maine Road and this time it was a pleasant one – who to leave out of the side.

Said Joe Mercer: "We played well there in the League Cup and lost. This time we were playing better, but had we not survived that particular period after Glyn Pardoe had put us one-up it could have been much more difficult. Then Chris Jones' exceptionally good goal gave us control."

The goal Joe Mercer was talking about was my first goal in League football. People still ask if I can remember it and my answer is always "vividly".

The best way to describe the goal is to go to the reporter's interview after the game who asked me to describe it

"I went for a return pass from Neil Young out on the left wing with Stan Jones (West Brom centre half) down by the line of the penalty area. Stan Jones overrode the ball in the tackle and I had the ball on the dead ball line. Williams came in and I dummied him. Then Stan Jones was back again but this was a desperate tackle and I got free. I was hoping all the time to find someone with a pull-back but I couldn't see anyone or hear anyone calling. I moved the ball out a bit from the line and then saw that the goalkeeper had come off the line and sold himself to his left and I hit the ball in between him and his near post and into the net. At the time I was more pleased about the state of the game the goal came in rather than the goal itself."

Looking back from that report I was obviously streetwise enough to say the right things at the right time. However a few issues came to mind afterwards and one was that the captain Johnny Crossan was screaming for me to pull the ball back to him and I had "turned a deaf one" on him – he gave me a bollocking for it after the game. My intention as a goal scorer was always to look for the chance to score and the West Brom goalkeeper exposed his near post and gave me that opportunity. Stan Jones, the West Brom centre half, always remembered that I did him twice down the line before I scored when we reminisced about it when we both played for Walsall in 1971-72.

On Monday 12th December 1966 we travelled to Altrincham for a friendly match and Mike Summerbee was back in action after a two week suspension. Being a native son I hoped to get a rousing reception from the team I supported as a lad and only a stones' throw from Stamford Park and home. In the Altrincham side that night was Jack Swindells whom I had supported as a lad and Clive Colbridge who was an ex-Maine Road man playing on the left wing.

Altrincham had a 10,000 crowd for this friendly and if I thought I was going to get a warm reception from the Moss Lane end I was rudely awakened. I was booed vociferously every time I got the ball. It took the pressure off Mike who was having his first competitive outing and still managed to find time to have a go at the referee. He got lucky when Frank Cowan the referee didn't send him off for a few choice swear words after disallowing a goal from a free kick which Mike had smashed into the roof of the net. He had been sent off by referee Jim Carr in a home game against Newcastle on 5thNovember – fireworks of the wrong kind from Mike. We won 4-0 with Glyn Pardoe scoring twice and Johnny Crossan and Colin Bell the other goals.

I would like to have scored on my homecoming but a 4-0 win satisfied me and that Altrincham could watch a local boy make good.

With Neil Young injured I kept my place for the following game against Southampton at Maine Road and Mike Summerbee made his comeback. We drew 1-1 and Mike Summerbee got quite a bit of tap from Tony Knapp, obviously trying to get him sent off again. We didn't have much luck during the game with Glyn hitting the bar and Mike being blatantly pulled down in the box – but no penalty. The referee gave a free kick on the edge of the box as a compromise.

Southampton had a good side out that day with Terry Paine, Jimmy Melia and a very potent strike partnership in Martin Chivers and Ron Davies. It was Ron Davies who scored for the Saints and Colin Bell got our equaliser. The pitch was a mud-bath and it became a physical battle and we couldn't just get a winner.

Christmas of 1966 was approaching and we had back to back games against Sheffield Wednesday to play with an 11am kick off on Boxing Day and a trip to Hillsborough on the following day. The home game was cancelled because of frost and I was on the bench for the game at Hillsborough which we lost 1-0.

We travelled to Sunderland on New Year's Eve and lost 1-0 in the last minute and on Monday 2nd January 1967 I was back in the starting line-up for the rearranged game against Sheffield Wednesday in front of a surprisingly large crowd of 30,000 fans. It was a dour game on a pitch that was only just past fit due to heavy mud which had frosted over early in the day. It was a murky, misty, cold and nasty night with a pitch that wouldn't have been played on nowadays. As *Mirror* reporter Frank McGhee put it, "Neither side deserved a 'panning' as the conditions made it difficult to change direction or turn and the ball had always to be played the way the man was facing."

Johnny Crossan had to go off with a pulled muscle and Matt Grey came on to replace him. I remember putting Matt through for the only real chance of the night but with a clear run towards Peter Springett in goal, he blasted the ball over the bar.

After Sheffield Wednesday had beaten us on Boxing Day they had gone on to demolish title-chasing Chelsea 6-1 on the Saturday so they were full of confidence. The pitch, however, beat both sides and it was only memorable for it being my fourth appearance for Manchester City and we ended up 0-0.

I found myself out of the team for the following game against Arsenal at Highbury which we lost 1-0 and the match against Manchester United at Maine Road at the end of January 1967. That game was drawn 1-1 and I suddenly found myself back in the reserves as Mike Summerbee went to centre forward and Paul Hince got his chance on the wing. While I was out of contention for a place in the line-up City had a mixed bag of results in the League winning only two games, both 1-0, against Burnley and Blackpool at Maine Road and drawing six games by the end of March.

However in the FA Cup we had been winning games, beating Leicester City at the end of January 1967 in the third round 2-1at Maine Road and following that with a fourth round win against Cardiff City 2-1 at Maine Road. That was after a replay following a 1-1 draw at Ninian Park Cardiff.

I was starting to score at more than a goal a game in the reserves including a hat-trick against Manchester United at Maine Road, and felt that both Joe and Malcolm were taking note of my performances and also noting the lack of goals scored in the League games. The FA Cup games were taking a toll and I was lined up to play against West Bromwich Albion on the 25th March but in the end Paul Hince was again preferred in the team. He scored both goals at Maine Road in a 2-2 draw but a convincing win in the League was still eluding the team.

Three days later I was called up into the squad for our away game against Leicester City whom we had lost to 3-1 at Maine Road the week previous. Malcolm had hinted that I would get a game and positions were up for grabs for the Sheffield United game in the League and the FA Cup quarter-final against Leeds United at Elland Road on the 8th April.

At Leicester City I was again disappointed but had the consolation of reaching the substitutes' bench. Leicester had a very good side in 1967 including Mike Stringfellow, Dave Gibson, Jackie Sinclair, Jimmy Goodfellow and the legendary Gordon Banks in goal.

Gordon was one of the heroes of England's World Cup success over West Germany in 1966 but this was to be one of his last games for Leicester City, as Matt Gillies and the Board of Directors saw fit to ignominiously ditch him for a young goalkeeper called Peter Shilton.

In the cruel world of professional football, no player's position was safe even for the world-nominated second best goalkeeper of the 20th century. Gordon was told that Gillies thought his best footballing days were behind him and that an ultimatum by Shilton to the directors had forced his hand into getting rid of one of the Country's footballing heroes. Over the hill or not, Banks was to go on and play in the next World Cup in Mexico in 1970 and make that legendary save from a Pele header , diving down to his right and flicking the ball up and over the bar. Unfortunately he got food poisoning after that game and Peter Bonnetti took over in goal. Later an eye accident finished Gordon's career but not before he was named in 1971 as the Football Writers' Footballer of the Year, the first goalkeeper to receive the honour since Bert Trautmann of Manchester City had received the same honour in 1956.

It was a wet Tuesday evening at Filbert Street when we played Leicester City. They had a talented side and kept us on defence in the first half with Mike Stringfellow who had taken over from Derek Dougan the main threat with his pace down the middle. Alan Ogley was in our goal and he made a string of saves before Jackie Sinclair flicked it over George Heslop's head and volleyed it in as the ball dropped at his feet. Tony Book sustained a leg injury before half time and I came on for my first game in eight weeks, determined to make the most of my chance. Whether it was me or just that we had to chase the game, Manchester City became the more aggressive side and for most of the second half we laid siege to Gordon Bank's goal.

As sometimes happens a team can break away on the counter-attack and Leicester City managed to do this to us. Jackie Sinclair scored his second in the 73rd minute and the game was nearly up for us. However we had a never give-up mentality at Manchester City and we poured forward looking at least for a consolation goal. With seven minutes to go Johnny Crossan centred from the right wing and I got in front of Graham Cross and flung myself at the ball. My diving header flew past Gordon Banks for one of my most memorable goals and one that I will always cherish against the man I consider as the World's best goalkeeper of that time.

I nearly equalised in the last minute with a strong right foot shot just as Cross put his studs into my ankle. The final whistle went and disappointed as I was at not winning I knew I had scored a memorable goal and that I had put myself in the frame for the next League game, and a possible FA Cup quarter-final against Leeds United.

As I walked off the field I thought my boot sounded squelchy and I looked down to see my sock soaked in blood. I showed Harty and the Doctor was called to see what was wrong. The result was a swift trip to the medical room where I had four stitches inserted into a horizontal cut right across the ankle bone, which was very painful as there was no skin for the stitches and I had to hop back onto the bus.

Malcolm had been elated by my performance and said that he hoped I might train in a few days. I hoped so too as two big games were coming up but I tried to look more confident than I felt and could see this late injury keeping me out for quite a while. I missed the game against Sheffield United having failed a fitness test on the Friday when Malcolm tried to get me to run up and down the running track. The ankle was strapped but I knew there was no way I could play the following day. I did my best, but it was foolhardy and I had burst the wound open again and my dreams of an FA Cup match the following week against Leeds United had disappeared.

I was out for three weeks with the injury and again became the forgotten man of the squad and ended up playing the last weeks of the season in the Central League team.

We lost the quarter-final against Leeds 1-0 at Elland Road and the season finished with the team getting three wins and three draws during the last month to finish 15th in the Division. Tottenham and Chelsea were to go on to compete in the Cup final that year with Tottenham beating Chelsea 2-1. I found I was not quite forgotten by Malcolm and Joe and was preferred to Ralph Brand as a squad member and selected for our close season tour of Germany which gave a great boost to my confidence.

HISTORY BOYS OF 1967-1968

Manchester urbem prima quia vindices 1936-1937
Manchester City as First Division Champions since 1936-37

The close season came to an end in the middle of May and the Club exercised its option to retain me. A small pay rise was offered as well as the incentives of crowd and win bonuses if I was in the team. However as there were only 12 places up for selection for each game (the days of only one substitute), picking up some extra cash was difficult. Dave Connor, being a versatile player, was always preferred to the other squad members as substitute. Many was the time I joined the first team at the Grand in Manchester for pre-match meals and then told I was not wanted and to join up with the reserves.

At the end of the season, came the close season tour of West Germany and Belgium. We were all fitted out in new Club suits and I started to feel that maybe I was making progress with Joe and Malcolm.

We travelled down to London to watch Mike Summerbee play for England on the Friday night and the Cup final on the Saturday. Malcolm did not travel with us on the day and the rumour had it that he was talking to Juventus representatives in the Midlands about a new job. However he was with us for the Cup final and flew out with us to Germany on the Sunday.

Our first game against West German side Eintracht Braunschweig was a challenge match to kick off British Week in the West German town of Gutersloh. I thought that our old friend from the Manchester City days Bert Trautmann would have been pleased to see soccer transgress the boundaries after what had happened 25 year before between the two countries.

Eintracht Braunshweig were founder members of the Bundesliga in 1963 and where we had Manchester United as our main rivals, they had Hanover 96. They won the title just after losing 2-1 to us in Gutersloh and relied on a solid defensive formation and a top class goalkeeper in Horst Wolter, who let in only 27 goals during the season. Well I added two goals to that list and we thought we may have dented their championship hopes.

The match was played in quite a quaint football stadium, with a capacity 12,000 crowd hoping to see the side which was just two points off winning the German Bundesliga title give us a good hammering. I remember the game was played in searing heat and that their goalkeeper Horst Wolter was also the West German International goalkeeper at the time and played 13 times for his Country

We were a goal down in the first half before I equalised early in the second. According to Peter Gardner of the *Manchester Evening News* the goal I scored after an hour to win the match was a "world-beating" affair which gave the Blues a sensational victory. Well, my two goals for Manchester City in the previous season took some beating, as did the diving header against Gordon Banks and my dribble along the touchline to score my debut goal at West Bromwich Albion. However in the context of beating the West German champions and Joe and Malcolm's determination to knock the arrogance out of them,it was certainly a bit special. My mate Tadger (Harty's nickname for Dave Connor) slung over a 30 yard pass into the box and I hit it on the volley into Wolter's top right hand corner. German International or not, he had no chance. As I turned to celebrate I thought *This gives the management something to think about.*

At that moment the announcer said: "Der Torschutze ist Mike Summerbee" (the goalscorer is Mike Summerbee). At that I ran towards the announcer on the half way line, pointed to my number and said, "Nicht, der Torschutze ist Chris Jones!"Mike Doyle said, "What did you say, CMNJ? Are you talking Kraut?" (when he was being clever Doyley always used to go to my initials).

Cockily I retorted: "Get a Grammar school education, Mike". To which his reply was, as always, "Grammar school Twat" Limited grammar and eloquence from Doyley, as always'.

Still, it was a great moment for me as we moved on to Aachen for our second game of the tour against Standard Liege and we won that 2-1.

Tony Coleman had been signed towards the end of the 1966/67 football season from Doncaster Rovers and was a bit of wild boy with a bad footballing reputation. However Malcolm liked characters and had let Joe Mercer know he could handle him.

TC, as we called him, said if he scored he didn't want all that namby-pamby stuff of hugging and kissing and, you guessed it, he scored. Good team spirit was growing in the team as we all chased Tony down to hug him and kiss him. The foreign supporters must have wondered what was going on, as grown men chased a team mate half way across the pitch to congratulate him.

The team finished the tour in high spirits (unlike the following season's tour in America) and as I left Manchester to go to Malta I had high hopes of starting the pre-season in the team and holding my place for the first game of the season.

We beat Borussia Dortmund in a pre-season friendly. Johnny Crossan had been sold to Middlesbrough and I was one of three players ear-marked to take his place, John Clay and Bobby Kennedy being the other two in the squad for selection.

In the practice game on the Tuesday I was in the First team but didn't feel too well. I had got a touch of tonsillitis, but, not thinking it was too bad, stayed at home in Altrincham and as we were off on the Wednesday decided not to let the Club know. By Thursday I felt OK and trained with the team and everything seemed well. On Friday it was still in doubt which one of the three of us would start the game. Malcolm and Joe gave nothing away but I was still favourite to play against Liverpool. My concern was: had I fully recovered from my bad throat and should I report it? I kept quiet, trained well on the Friday and was given the nod to start in the all-ticket match against Liverpool.

Fifty thousand ecstatic fans were in the ground at the start of the campaign which would see Manchester City win the First Division title for the first time since 1936.

Tommy Smith and Emlyn Hughes were in the line-up with Roger Hunt and Tony Hateley in the attack. It was a dour and uncompromising battle of two sides, a jarring encounter of true professionalism. The big moment of the game came in the 73rd minute when Neil Young flipped the ball over Tommy Smith's head and was mown to the ground in the box. We had no regular penalty taker as John Crossan was on the move to Middlesbrough and our new skipper Tony Book stepped up to take it.

Tony, Mr Cool on all occasions, ambled in and calmly put the ball over the bar. It was a hard encounter with defences on top and I giving it out to the likes of Hughes and Smith with no quarter asked or give. The foul count was high on both sides and I think both Managers were glad to come away with a point in a 0-0 draw. I only had one chance to score, from a cross by TC which Neil Young should have hit it but dummied and it hit me on the shin from eight yards out and went into Tommy Lawrence's hands. I was out of the side after that match and wondered if we had won whether I would have held my place The next two games were away and I lost my place to a more defensive side for the away games which we lost against Southampton 3-2 at the Dell and Stoke City 3-0 at the Victoria ground.

Instead of getting my place back Stan Bowles and Paul Hince were tried in the team and Mike Summerbee moved to centre forward. It was getting harder to get a game as the team won the next five games and I was back into the reserves – though still scoring goals.

We lost the next two games against Arsenal 1-0 at Highbury and everybody at the Club was mortified when Manchester United beat us 2-1 at Maine Road.

Joe signed Francis Lee from Bolton Wanderers for £60,000 and the Holy Trinity of Lee, Bell, and Summerbee was complete as the side settled down to compete for the Championship. I was still battling for recognition but it was a forlorn hope as we won eight and drew two of the next ten games as Christmas approached. Back in the reserves I was still scoring until things went from bad to worse.

I was playing in a Lancashire Senior Cup match at Oldham Athletic on a wet, cold and greasy night at the end of November 1967. I went into a slide tackle after about half an hour of the game and my left leg went all askew and lay at an awful angle. Paul Hince always seemed to be the first there and I said, "For fuck's sake Paul put it back in and get me up." Paul always tells it that it was the bravest thing he had seen on a football field but it was just a complete shock causing that reaction.

Paul then said, "Don't look at it Jonesy," which was the last thing to say as I took one glance and my stomach turned over. All I could think was I would never play again as it looked horrific. Paul was as white as me as Dave Ewing raced on to the pitch and threw a towel over the leg. I was in pain and shock as the stretcher took me back to the dressing room. Believe it or not, in a way it was my lucky night, as in the crowd was Sidney Rose, a Director of Manchester City who was a doctor and surgeon. Sidney had attended to Bert Trautmann when he broke his neck in the 1956 Cup final and later probably saved Glyn Pardoe's leg when an artery was trapped in that awful tackle with George Best at Old Trafford in 1971. I knew him best for treating my Aunt Hazel's varicose veins.

Sidney, who sadly passed away in 2014, was responsible for the welfare of the City players and at the top of his profession. He was on the Board for over 25 years and was granted the prestige title of Life Vice President of the Club. Thank goodness that he was there that night and probably saved my career.

The dressing room at Boundary Park is low-ceilinged with just a bed in the centre. I was put on that and Sidney Rose was there next to Peter Blakey, our physio, who looked even whiter than Paul Hince.

Mr Rose said, "Chris you have a dislocation of the knee but if you can stand some pain I could put it back for you now. It would be better than sending you up to the infirmary as the sooner it is back in could reduce the length of time you will be out of action." Confident and soothing words from Mr Rose, and the thought that my career was not going to be ruined, gave me the nerve to say, "Put it back Sidney, I am in pain as it is." A swift movement from the capable hands of Mr Rose and it went back in and Peter Blakey had the splints and support bandages ready and I was feeling a lot better as I slumped back on the bed.

Mr Rose didn't mention the possibility of cruciate damage or cartilage problems and just said to give it a few days and then he would check the swelling and any necessity for X-rays and possible surgery at the Manchester Royal Infirmary.

An announcement went out for my mate Roger Green who was in the ground to come to the players' entrance. Roger turned up and Malcolm asked if he could get me home. Malcolm gave Roger a tenner for his trouble, the equivalent of a week's wages for him at the time.

Well, I will always be thankful to Sidney Rose, a real gentleman whom I had the pleasure of meeting again at the Etihad Stadium at a Former Players' dinner in 2011. When I saw him at the Manchester Royal Infirmary the X-rays showed I had got away with just some ligament damage and he told me I would be back in training in the New Year. I would have to do a lot of hard work on the quadriceps and calf muscles to build the left leg up, but it should be as good as new. A fortnight later I was still on crutches but in for physio and leg exercises.

Roger used to drop me off and pick me up at dinner time for the trip back to Altrincham.

I was sat on the step outside the player's entrance waiting for my lift when Joe and Malcolm started to come down the main steps from the offices when a police car raced up, sirens wailing and lights flashing as it rushed towards the ground.

I heard Joe say to Malcolm, "What have you been fucking up to now, Mal?"

"Nothing Joe, I can't understand it."

"Well what about TC or Bowlesy, have they been up to anything lately?"

"Not as far as I know."

I was by then trying to catch Joe and Malcolm's attention. "Hey Boss, I think it's for me."

Mal said, "What have you done, hit somebody with your fucking crutch?"

Just then a policeman got out of the car, put his helmet on and trotted out the traditional copper's greeting: "Hello, hello, hello!"

Of course Mal then recognised it was my mate Roger who he had met a few weeks earlier when he was out of uniform. Relief all round, though I groaned at him taking the piss out of the Manager and Coach.

Malcolm and Joe must have recognised my determination to get back into the reckoning and a few weeks later as I recuperated I was taken with the first team to Southport for a couple of training days on the sand dunes. These were tough sessions and Harty and Dave had no mercy on me as they pushed and gave me the confidence to overcome what I saw as a career threatening injury. Even today, over 45 years later, I give my left knee a rub and thank my lucky stars that Sidney Rose, a top man in his profession and one of life's gentlemen, was in the ground at Oldham Athletic on that night back in 1967.

Mike Summerbee was on International duty for England on the 24th February 1968 and I had been back playing in the reserves since the start of the month. I was starting to play well again and scoring a few goals when I was drafted back into to the first team against Sunderland at Maine Road.

This, as it turned out, was going to be my last first team appearance for Manchester City. On a mud heap of a pitch we managed to win a dour affair 1-0 and Francis Lee scored the goal which gave us both points. The season came to an end with the First Division Championship in our hands after a 4-3 win at Newcastle United at St James' Park on the 11th May 1968. I did not play in the game but was privileged to be in the dressing room at the end of the match to join in the celebrations of our first League Championship since 1937.

The First Division trophy was not at Newcastle on the day which was a let let-down for the squad and we had to wait until the following Tuesday when a special game was arranged at Bury for us to receive the Cup. Having played in only two games in the League that season (Liverpool and Sunderland) I was not entitled to a League Winners' medal. I thought to myself that this was a shame as the games I played in garnered three valuable points for the team in what was a very close finish to the campaign, only won in the last minutes of the season. Looking back it gives me a lot of satisfaction that I never started a game for Manchester City and lost and but for injuries would have made a lot more appearances for the Club.

MANCHESTER CITY'S TOUR OF AMERICA AND MY EXIT FROM THE CLUB

AMERICAN FOOTBALL IN 1967 AND 1968

At the end of the 1967 season the owners of the USA and NPSL league clubs found themselves 500,000 dollars in the red and tried to analyse what had gone wrong with their investments in soccer. If they had asked the soccer fans the answers were clear, but they didn't.

The answer was that Americans knew little about soccer or its great teams and players. The Americans found the two leagues producing a boring and slow product and stuck with their baseball and American football.

The owners of the teams had also overestimated the effects of the previous season's World Cup in 1966. Sports fans in America were not about to rush out and buy season tickets as they would for their beloved American football and baseball.

I actually watched a double-header baseball match in Atlanta, home of the Braves and found it boring. However they did have a legend playing in Hank Aaron and he alone was worth the admission money, if I had paid. I have actually got his autographed bat in my home to this day.

By 1968 it should have been clear to all that a slow track to growth would have to be followed with an eye to educating and entertaining the American fans, preferably from home-grown stars.

The owners of the clubs were not concerned with what the American community thought or what the problems were. All they wanted was a simple explanation for their failure and they found one.

It was not any of the above miscalculations or the brand of Soccer offered that caused the heavy financial losses. Nor was it the hurried planning or numerous high-salaried administrators or advisors. Neither did they consider it could be the inept recruiting of both players and coaches.

A lot of the early recruiting was of players who could not make it in the Football League and similar leagues in Europe and South America. The coaches just had an FA coaching badge and they were looking for a new beginning in football.

In the minds of the owners the fault lay in the unnecessary competition of the two Leagues which had diluted the support of the fans. They decided to give the Country one Professional League and they believed that attendances would escalate.

So in December 1967 the two Leagues merged and formed the North American Soccer League (NASL), taking the original name of the USA groups.

Of the 27 franchises in the league only 17 were retained. A certain amount of shuffling of the teams was necessary to prevent any two teams from competing against one another for support. Chicago's franchise moved to Kansas City and Los Angeles re-located to San Diego. New York Skyliner's folded to make way for the Generals and San Francisco yielded to Oakland Raiders.

The owners of the Golden Gate Gales subsequently purchased a controlling interest in the Vancouver Royals while Philadelphia and Pittsburgh's franchises folded because of horrendous debts.

With the new arrangements only thirty North American footballers were found to be good enough to play at professional level and they were sprinkled among the 17 teams. Recognising the lack of talent and desire in the league players were recruited from overseas. John Kowalik was the MVP player of the year so far, Ruben Navarro was recruited by the Washington Whips and San Diego acquired Vava the Brazilian International star of the 1962 World Cup.

At the same time in early 1968 Ferenc Puskas, star of Hungary and Real Madrid, was brought in to coach the Vancouver Royals. However the difficulty was that the Royals were already committed to Bobby Robson as Coach.

The problem arose as Puskas was originally in Canada to coach San Francisco in 1968. Once the franchise moved to Vancouver one of the two men had to step down. Bobby Robson was offered the job of assistant to Puskas and promptly resigned.

In 1968 the calibre of players and play reached a level of quality that would not be seen in North America for another ten years.

Not only Manchester City would learn the hard way that the sides were no push-overs. Both Cleveland Stokers and New York Generals would defeat Pele and his Santos team from Brazil.

Manchester United also lost three games to the Atlanta Chiefs 3-2 and 2-1 and to the Oakland Clippers 3-1.

Malcolm Allison treated the NASL as a joke and stated that the Atlanta Chiefs were no better than a Fourth Division outfit. Ex-pats players and a sprinkling of Internationals from overseas playing in America were not going to allow that slight to go unpunished.

Following my disappointment at not managing to force myself into the First team for the run in to our League Championship, my selection to tour America gave me the feeling that I was still in Joe and Malcolm's plans for the following season and I was going to take the opportunity to impress.

However the tour was like a celebration for the regular first team players and we were missing Colin Bell and Mike Summerbee on International duties with England. Mike Doyle was missing for a young England game and Alan Oakes did not travel for personal reasons.

The Tour would become arduous with injuries, and nine matches arranged against Dunfermline, Borussia Dortmund and the newly formed North American League sides Rochester Lancers and Atlanta Chiefs. The itinerary would have us playing nine games spread over Canada, USA and Mexico.

We flew into Toronto after an eight hour flight to be greeted with nearly 80 degrees of heat, a lot warmer than when we left chilly Manchester. The hotel we stayed at was a magnificent 160 bedroom place and the City of Toronto put on a civic lunch for us. Eric Morecambe of Morecambe and Wise fame joined us and kept the lads in stitches. He was appearing in a show in the City but kept us entertained over lunch.

Toronto looked after us very well and arranged a trip to Niagara Falls which was quite a magnificent spectacle. Francis Lee was heard to say, "They have something similar in Westhoughton." The following morning Harry Dowd, Dave Connor and me thought we would go out for breakfast. We ordered up and when it arrived we were presented with four eggs and numerous rashers of bacon and pancakes. It was enough to feed the whole squad and definitely not a pre-match meal. We didn't tell Malcolm Allison or Joe Mercer.

Our first game was against Dunfermline who were the Scottish Cup winners that year. Any thought that George Farm, their Manager, was going to allow the game to be a bit of an exhibition proved to be false as his team set up shop to defend and play on the break. We drew 1-1 in front of 10,000 fans. Most, I think, had come to see Malcolm Allison and Tony Book who had both played for Toronto City in 1964. We were a goal down at half time to a dubious penalty but came out well in the second half and Neil Young equalised after a minute running through a square defence to beat goalkeeper Bent Martin. I had a chance to win the game but unfortunately took a divot and the shot went wide.

After the game we flew straight to New York arriving at three in the morning and checked into the Sheraton-Atlantic Hotel. At 10.30 we were off again in the coach to play Dunfermline again, this time in New Britain, Connecticut

Once more George Farm refused to open the game out, saying his team's reputation was on the line and he didn't see why he should play an expansive game. As before, we had difficulty breaking down a stubborn defence and went a goal down again. Glyn Pardoe equalised.

As Malcolm was trying to keep us going on the touchline, Glyn shouted, "I bet our kid [Alan Oakes, his cousin who had not come with us] is just driving off down the fifth at Sandiway." Back came the retort from at least three players, "And I wish I was with him". Actually the language was a lot stronger and more descriptive than that.

Quite a place New York, as Neil Young and George Heslop would have testified. They had seen a movie on Broadway and decided to go into a bar for a drink. As they approached the door a squad of policemen rushed out. It seems that they had been only minutes behind a double murder bid with a fellow having shot his girl and the waiter in the bar. They came back to the hotel shaken and said it seemed like a scene from Frankie and Johnny.

Three days later we had moved on to Rochester to play the Lancers. At last the shackles were off and we were allowed to show some of the football that had won us the League a month earlier. We won the game 4-0 and Francis Lee turned on the style and scored all four. We had a strong side out this time with me leading the attack with Francis Lee on the right wing. Neil Young, Tony Coleman and Stan Bowles making up a very attack-minded side.

The difficult part of the Tour was that we were regally welcomed everywhere and concentrating on the training necessary to keep up the standards was very harrowing. You have to remember that City were like every other club on tour, wanting to enjoy the experience of a new Country. Air travel, receptions, training and playing against different oppositions took it out on an already weary squad.

Malcolm and Joe were great ambassadors and the team backed them up to the hilt. However Malcolm, in a country which could match his ego, was garrulous and put us on the spot when we arrived in Atlanta to play the Chiefs in the Braves' stadium. The hotel and the receptions put on for the team were spectacular and a little bit of me thought they were ripening us up for a sacrifice against the Chiefs who'd had this game on their radar for quite a while. They had been advertising the game for weeks to attract one of the biggest soccer crowds to the stadium. One of the stunts had the team riding through Atlanta on horseback shouting "the British are coming".

We were taken out on a trip to the theme park Six Flags over Georgia on the Chattahoochee River. It was spectacular but not what we really needed in an approach to a game against the Atlanta Chiefs. It was very tiring, another reception, a trip on the river boat and then back to Atlanta for the match.

I was proved right, as over 25,000 were in the stadium to see if their team could take the Manchester City scalp. It had been 80 degrees Fahrenheit during the day and the humidity in Atlanta was around

80 per cent. For footballers travelling around the Country at the end of a long season and being royally entertained this was going to be a tough night.

The Atlanta team was managed by Phil Woosnam, the former Welsh International and Aston Villa player, and we were in for a hard game as the Chiefs treated it like a Cup-Final, American style.

Both teams came out behind National flags, the spotlights were turned on the teams while the National Anthems were played and then each of us kicked a football into the stands round the ground. Every player was announced individually and waved to the crowd to plenty of cheer.

When Bobby Kennedy was announced they all booed and it was only later that we realised that Senator Bobby Kennedy on the campaign trail was not liked around Atlanta, Georgia.

The Chiefs ran the tired legs off our team and managed to come out 3-2 winners. Tony Coleman had given us the lead but Graham Newton, an English exile, equalised and they scored two late goals before Francis Lee scored from the penalty spot. Malcolm was spitting feathers and tried to say they were lucky – one of the goals was scored by a player four yards offside and we would drub them if we played them again. The truth is that the Chiefs had a good team and won the League and the play-off final that year. They would also go on to beat Manchester United twice, so as it turned out, considering we were short of some of our star players, the result wasn't quite as disastrous as Malcolm made out.

Malcolm, however, took the defeat as a personal affront and as we flew out of Atlanta heading for Chicago he was already trying to work out if we could have a revenge match with the Chiefs.

From the players point of view that was the last thing on our minds as the tour was not only sapping our strength but injuries were piling up as we looked to play Borussia Dortmund. We had thrashed them in a pre-season friendly 5-0 at Maine Road, but they were really the last team we wanted to play coming off a defeat by Atlanta Chiefs, especially as Chicago was a German stronghold in America.

Well, we played OK and put in a good performance but in front of nearly 9,000 fans all supporting Borussia Dortmund we lost 2-1.

By the time we flew out of Chicago for Vancouver we had played five games in 12 days – unheard of in the modern game. In Vancouver we played Dunfermline for the third time and the game was even more boring for the 6,500 fans than our last two efforts.

George Farm again refused to play any form of attacking football and with Barry at the back (later at Coventry City) marshalling a dour defence neither side could score. It was like attack versus defence and we were completely frustrated by the games we played against them. There was more action in the emergency ward than there was on the field. Neil Young was carried off after just five minutes and rushed to hospital after a horrific tackle which needed 24 stitches in a shin wound and two days' bed rest before he was flown home with Stan Horne. Stan Bowles followed Neil to hospital from the same game to have eight stitches put in a head wound and Stan Horne finished the game with tendon trouble. With Dave Connor having treatment, we were down to ten fit players by the time we flew to Los Angeles for yet another game against Dunfermline.

This time we were going to have a result as we had agreed on penalties as there was a Cup up for grabs. This incentive didn't bother George Farm who refused to let the game have a few goals for both teams and then play on from there. You guessed it: the game ended 0-0 and both teams got the slow-handclap from the 5,000 fans, but we had the last laugh, taking the game on penalties.

Tony Coleman was given the task of taking the penalties for City against Ian Lister for Dunfermline. Tony kept his nerve and won 6-5 on sudden death. Unfortunately the game was very physical and bad tempered. I think familiarity bred contempt and we as a team had had enough of George Farm trying to prove a point.

Well, we won that game for Neil Young but none of us was enjoying playing against the Scots. To this day that was the worst injury I have seen from studs and it needed internal stitching before they could add external ones. We had just twelve fit players for the game including Ken Mulhearn in goal and Harry Dowd as our substitute. The rest of the team was made up of Tony Book, Glyn Pardoe, Bobby Kennedy, George Heslop, Jimmy Mundy, Francis Lee, Stan Bowles, me, Dave Connor and Tony Coleman.

In Los Angeles we were staying at the Hollywood Roosevelt Hotel, and Senator Robert Kennedy, the brother of the assassinated John Kennedy, was also in Los Angeles, speaking at the Ambassador Hotel a mile away.

Just after midnight when we were all in our hotel rooms, Robert Kennedy was shot as he walked through the kitchen of the Ambassador Hotel. On television we just heard a commentator saying that something had happened at the back of the Hotel and he believed a shot had been fired at the Senator and hit him.

John Hart knocked on our door to see if we had seen what happened. He then said we had better tell the Chairman, Albert Alexander. Albert was a wonderful guy, small in stature and very religious. He always went to bed early. John knocked on the door and a figure appeared half asleep in a night-gown.

Sleepily Albert asked what was wrong and John said Bobby Kennedy had been shot. Albert's reply was, "What was he doing out of his room, John, we were all supposed to be in our rooms?"

John said not our Bobby Kennedy, Senator Robert Kennedy. The reply came dreamily. "Well that's all right then, good night." He shut the door and went back to bed.

So our Chairman, master of the understatement, let history pass him by: as long as our player Bobby Kennedy was OK that satisfied him.

Robert Kennedy was mortally wounded as he was taken to the Good Samaritan Hospital in Los Angeles. Our game was still played but a sense of history was all around the city as everyone awaited news of the Senator. Robert Kennedy died 26 hours after the shooting and we heard that a man called Sirhan Sirhan had been arrested for the assassination. Kennedy's body lay in repose for two days in Saint Patrick's before his funeral Mass. His body was interred near his brother's John in Arlington Cemetery.

By that time we had left Los Angeles and headed for San Francisco before playing the Oakland Clippers. Mike Doyle, especially flown over for the final part of the tour after playing in an under-23 International for England, had joined us in San Francisco which would help to give some relief to what was now a depleted squad.

We had a crowd of over 25,000, the biggest ever to watch a game in California, and trouble flared in the mid-day heat. We went a goal down and our players' tempers, already on a short fuse after the events with Dunfermline, boiled over. Tony Coleman took a swing at Oakland Clippers full back Gavric who went down faster than one of Muhammed Ali's opponents. The American referee Ed Tearson sent TC off in the 31st minute and three minutes later he sent off Mike Doyle too, for swearing at him.

I think by then events had overtaken our ambitions to win the game and we duly lost 3-1 in the mid-day heat of nearly a 100 degrees. Jack Charlton was to take his Republic of Ireland team there at a later World Cup, and wanted stops for water due to dehydration.

We were literally thrown to the lions and completely shredded, with half the squad injured or walking wounded. The heat just finished us off and Malcolm and Joe didn't have much to say to the Press afterwards.

The Tour was having too much bad luck and wasn't worth the loss of Stan and Neil. Defeats were becoming hard to take and Malcolm was still looking for that one moment which could turn the tour into a success.

San Francisco was a fascinating City to stay in with Fisherman's Wharf and Alcatraz not to be missed. It was also the time of the beautiful people and flower power. The 1967 hit San Francisco by Scott McKenzie (*Be sure to wear some flowers in your hair*) was on everybody's lips during June of 1968. This was my Uncle Bill's favourite record over the years and the song I always associate it with him to this day.

For the connoisseur, the musicians that played on *San Francisco* were Joe Osborne, a member of The Wrecking Crew (who were studio musicians and ended up in the R&R Hall of Fame – Hal Blaine on drums and keyboardist Larry Knechtel, who became part of Bread with singer David Gates). The fourth member of the Wrecking Crew was none other than Glen Campbell. However, Glen was not on that record and it was John Phillips of The Mamas and the Papas (who wrote *San Francisco*) who played on the record at that session instead.

We flew 2,000 miles to play two games against Necaxa and Atlante in Mexico. But the promoters claimed that Manchester City could not comply with their contract, not having 15 fit players available. Injuries had also taken out Francis Lee, George Heslop and Stan Bowles. The games were called off.

But we had a fabulous few days in Mexico and did a bit of training at altitude. We also realised that the next World Cup in 1970 was to be in Mexico and had a taste at first-hand of what playing at altitude would be like. Joe was to report back to the FA on the conditions and effects on training at the altitude, so the trip was not completely futile.

In Mexico City Malcolm was thinking about revenge on Atlanta Chiefs. He arranged through Phil Woosnam that we would fly back to Atlanta to play them again. However the squad was very depleted and we were playing a very strong side of ex-pats and players from South America, so we were on a hiding to nothing. We lost 2-1 and I had our goalkeeper Harry Dowd playing centre forward with me. In front of a record 26,000 crowd we conceded two goals before I managed to pull one back shortly before the end

That final result may have soured Malcolm towards the fringe players in our squad and although I personally had had a reasonable tour, scoring five goals in our nine games, Malcolm came back in a bad mood. We had not taken the USA by storm and our players were shattered and needing a long rest to recuperate. Malcolm's boast that Manchester City would take Europe by storm in the following season probably slipped away after an exhilarating but tiring tour.

When we returned to Manchester I plane hopped and flew to Malta to become engaged to Therese whom I had met there two years previously.

That had been in 1966 the year we last won the World Cup and Bill and Hazel and myself had ventured away from the British Isles for a holiday for the first time. Why we chose Malta I have no idea but we fancied a surety of some warm sunshine and a good hotel with a swimming pool. I always remember that we had to change at Rome on our way as the plane did not carry enough fuel for the trip right through.

Anyway, we arrived in Malta and were staying in the Plevna Hotel in Sliema with the poolside down the road. We were to have our reception three years later around the Plevna swimming pool). But that was for the future: in 1966 I was a shy young lad when it came to chatting up the girls. At Reception were two girls, one of whom I fancied but I was too shy to approach – so much for the brave centre forward. Aunt Hazel came to the rescue.

I said, "Nip up to Reception and ask the dark haired girl if she wants to go to the beach with us after work."

Haze replied, "They are both dark haired – which one do you mean?"

"I'll tell you what," I said, "go up to Reception and stand near one of the girls and look back at me, if I nod it's the right one, OK?

Haze went up to Reception and looked back. I shook my head and she then went and asked the other girl the question, and when I saw her smile I decided it was time to take over. That was how I first met Therese and she did go to the beach with us that afternoon.

Therese told me not so long ago that she had another date for the afternoon with an Irish lad, which she broke to go out with me. I believe he was waiting outside at two o'clock and she ducked down behind the counter in Reception and sneaked out via the back way through the kitchens to meet me.

I tell the story to my in-laws who are both Irish. They laugh and say Therese took second best and should have gone with the Irish lad. Well, they got the next best thing as Francesca, my youngest, married Neil McClure in 2013 at St Wilfred's Church in York. As I said in my speech at the reception at Castle Howard afterwards, "a Prince with his Princess in his Castle." Neil is a good footballer, unfortunately with an oval ball and I now have had to learn Union rules and understand another game.

Well, I did return to Malta the following year and we stayed with Iris Camilleri, Therese's mother, in Lija. Therese's father Vincent had died in 1963 and Therese had left school at 15 to get a part-time job and help her mother look after the seven younger children. My father Lea had passed away in 1964 and so both Therese and I had early tragedy in the family. Therese came to visit us in Altrincham the following winter before I was back in Malta in 1968, by which time the family had moved to St Julian's. We were engaged that year and were setting up plans for the wedding in Malta 1969.

Meanwhile I had become a bit of a father figure for the young Camilleri family growing up in Malta. I spent £10, half my signing-on fee for the new season, on a small rowing boat for them – a lot of money at the time – and it gave them much pleasure throughout the summer school breaks. One of Therese's brothers, Martin, kept the boat for many years keeping it maintained until somebody stole it. We are all still keeping an eye open in Malta just in case: it was a memento of the good times gone by.

These were happy times for all of us in Malta in 1968 as I thought that things at Manchester City were on the up for me and further chances would come my way in the first team.

But how things can change in football over a couple of weeks of the close season.

LEAVING MANCHESTER CITY 1968

Manchester urbem relicto, tristitia.

When we reported for pre-season training I had a feeling that things were not right between Malcolm Allison and me. Then came frequent reports in the *Manchester Evening News* of Malcolm Allison being interested in another centre forward at Bury called Bobby Owen. If they bought him, I would go down the pecking order and chances of getting a longer run in the first team would diminish even further.

To a young player who loved Manchester City and had fought his way up through trials, Lancashire League sides and Youth team success to the first team, this was a heart breaking body blow to my ambitions.

And who was the Manager at Maine Road, anyway? Since winning the league we were hearing less of Joe Mercer and a lot more of Malcolm Allison

Joe I considered a gentleman and a top class manager, but due to illness he needed somebody like Malcolm alongside. It was a great partnership but by the summer of 1969 the decline between the two men was just starting, although Manchester City did go on to win the FA Cup in 1969 and the League Cup and the European Cup Winners' Cup in 1970.

The *Manchester Evening News* was still full of the Club signing Booby Owen and I decided it was time to have a talk with Joe.

This was the Monday morning and it was the day when we had a really tough training session at Wythenshawe Park.

I stayed back and saw Joe in his office.

"Boss I keep seeing in the Press that you want to sign Bobby Owen from Bury, is that rumour or fact?"

Joe said, "Oh you know Malcolm, he takes a notion to want a certain player and he keeps pursuing it. He thinks Owen might add an alternative to the team as he is good in the air."

"So it's true then you are attempting to bring Owen to the Club?"

"No he – sorry, we – can't buy him as it would stretch the budget and you know Walter Griffith wouldn't allow it."

But Joe went on, "It's Malcolm's decision to get another centre forward but Son I want you to stay and challenge for the position".

"That's all well and good Boss but I am now hearing that certain League clubs want to buy me, so how does that affect the situation?"

"Well I want you to stay, we had a tough pre-season tour but I was impressed with your performances. Maybe Malcolm will put Bobby Owen on the back-burner for now."

I left the office not sure what to believe. Joe Mercer the diplomat had left me feeling that maybe the future was still at Maine Road but I felt an under- current of something a lot deeper starting to happen at the Club.

Feeling slightly nonplussed, but happier at Joe's backing for my situation. I left the office to pick up the car and drive to Wythenshawe Park to join up with the squad. I was thinking that Bobby Owen and me in the same squad wasn't feasible, but consoled myself that I was an all-round better player than Bobby and could stave off any challenge from him.

I was surprised to find that Malcolm had not already left for training and was standing near my car in the car park. I realised he was waiting for me to come out of Joe's office.

"Chris, can I cadge a lift with you?"

"Sure Mal," said I knowing now that he wanted to know what had occurred during my meeting with Joe.

"What did the Boss have to say?" was Malcolm's opening gambit.

"Oh so you know I have been in to see him then."

"Of course," said Malcolm," Joe and I always work as a team".

"Well Malcolm, the Boss said he wanted me to stay and fight for my position and that is what I am going to do. He even said that he had faith in what I could achieve even if you still wanted Bobby Owen."

Malcolm's cold response sent a dagger to my heart and destroyed my future at Manchester City. He just said coldly while staring out of the front window.

"I think you should leave."

My response was slow and calculating.

"You have just said that Joe and you work as a team, but the Boss has told me to stay and you over-ride him by saying I should leave. Who is in charge at this Club?"

Malcolm coldly repeated what he had said before.

"You should leave the Club."

I was not going out with a whimper, as that was not my style. Malcolm was formidable and aggressive but I wanted my say.

"Who do you think you are, Malcolm, Joe is the Boss at this Club and you are just the Coach".

Well, that was the spark which ignited Malcolm's anger and from cold and calculating he flared up in a rage.

"Joe might think he is the fucking Boss but I make the decisions on players who stay at this Club.

"You haven't a future hear and I will buy Bobby Owen. I suggest you talk to other clubs."

Malcolm was like a spoilt brat and lost it in that moment. As both our tempers were rising and we were trapped in the car on Princess Parkway I decided to make one last comment to rankle Malcolm, knowing my time at Manchester City was finished.

"Well Malcolm, when I get back from training I will go and see Joe and find out who the real fucking Boss is at Manchester City".

"You fucking do that".

We both fell into an icy silence and I realised Malcolm had let his guard down for the first time about becoming the Manager of Manchester City and he was not happy that at least one player was aware of his ambitions.

It would take another two years of success before the empire the Mercer Allison years had produced would crumble. As all dynasty's, they crumble from within and on that trip to Wythenshawe Park I was given the first insight into the decline and fall of City's greatest years.

Malcolm visualised himself as a great manager as well as the great Coach he undoubtedly was and this ego would lead to his downfall.

It was the last words Malcolm and I heatedly spoke to each other for 40 years until we met again at the Etihad stadium when the squad of 1968 were celebrated by the former players and friends. It was a pale shadow of the 'big Mal' I knew back in the 60's and although we sat and talked I am not sure he was too aware of all the things which were happening around him. (He sadly passed away in 2012). However I like to remember Malcolm as the effervescent coach who lit up Manchester City and was responsible for my development as a young Professional Footballer and not the heated words spoken in my Triumph Spitfire on the way to Wythenshawe Park that Monday morning in 1968.

Malcolm went back from training with one of the other players and, completely gutted, I made the trip back to Maine Road knowing my time at the Club was up. But I wanted to confront Joe Mercer one last time with the conversation Malcolm and I had in my car on the way to training.

Joe obviously expected me and I was ushered into his office.

"Boss, I have been talking to Malcolm and unfortunately it developed into a row between us. Malcolm says that when it comes to team matters and who goes and stays he is the Boss. He wants me to talk to other clubs. Correct me if I am wrong but I thought you are the Boss?"

Joe obviously knew about Malcolm's ambition to become Manager, but the time to confront Malcolm was not now. Obviously things were going well and one young player was going to be sacrificed to keep the tranquillity between the two of them. Unfortunately that was me.

Joe said in his diplomatic way, "Well Son, Malcolm is adamant he wants Bobby Owen and if you stay you are going to be under Malcolm and life could be hell for you."

This I already knew, as Malcolm had said he would freeze me out of playing for even the reserves.

Joe went on, "Chris, if you have had words with Malcolm you know he can become a bastard and never forgets. Probably it would be best if you talked to other clubs.

"Walter can contact some interested clubs for you. You understand we won't let you go for nothing – we want a good fee for you."

Well, it looked like Mercer and Allison had done a job on me and that they already had a club in the wings for me, and that would raise the capital to buy Bobby Owen.

Still, deep down to this day I see the malevolence in Malcolm's eyes and realised on that Monday: Malcolm had Joe Mercer firmly in his sights as his next prey. Malcolm railroaded me out of the Club I loved and where I had the privilege of pulling on the light blue Jersey (even to this day it thrills me to think of it).

Maybe I should have stuck it out, considering myself a better player than Owen. In retrospect, I should have at least talked to my mentors, Johnny Hart and Harry Godwin, and got their advice on what to do, but I talked to Swindon Town the following day and signed within the week.

BETWEEN TWO CITIES

Inter urbes

SWINDON TOWN 1968-1969

There is that saying about "Out of the frying pan and into the fryer" and my move to Swindon Town for £15,000 was certainly in that category. I roughly knew where Swindon was from Mike Summerbee and also knowing about Don Rogers through the Youth Cup exploits of 1964.

What I didn't realise until after I signed was that the Manager Danny Williams was under immense pressure from the Board as his side had massively under-achieved during the last season.

He had bought me unseen and I was to be the last throw of the dice for him as a manager. He told me later with a wry grin that I was there as the sacrificial lamb to take the flak from the crowd if things went wrong.

For a young player away from home for the first time, settling in "down South" after a gruelling tour of America was to become an ordeal.

I managed to get off to a reasonable start, playing against Morton at the County Ground, scoring one and made two others in a 3-3 draw. After that it was all downhill as poor form, maybe reaction to that arduous tour of America, bad luck and homesickness took its toll.

It was a strange coincidence that we played Morton in a friendly and gained promotion to the Second Division, and I played against Morton in a friendly when York City gained promotion to the Second Division in 1973-1974.

Luckily for my sanity in the first few months I found myself staying with Kate and Frank Strange on the Lawns estate in Swindon and along with their sons and next door neighbours Ken and Pauline Knox they made me welcome.

Every weekend I hopped it back up to Altrincham and was looking to find a club in the North who would put me out of my footballing misery.

The fans, however, gave me a really tough time, obviously disgruntled with the early showing of the team and finding an expensive newcomer for their spleen.

However my early career had taught me a few things about the game and my attitude was to dig in and make things happen to try and win the fans over. Not easy, but I persevered.

However the more I tried the more I seemed to come up with some error that got the crowd going. Most of my games came from the subs' bench and 20 minutes of football was not long enough to win them over, especially as I knew the fans were waiting for me to make an error and get on my back.

However, with most teams I played for, success seemed to follow and it was no different for Swindon Town.

We had beaten Torquay United 2-1 in the League Cup and we won three and drew three of our League games but as I had not scored and we had three 0-0 draws; the fans were disgruntled every time I was on the ball.

Williams put me on the bench after that and on my first game back against Torquay in the League I strained the medial ligaments in my ankle. I had to watch as the team went on to fight their way through to the League Cup final by mid-December. For the record they defeated Bradford City after a replay and Blackburn Rovers in September of 1968 and needed replays against Coventry City and Derby County by early November of that year. All this time I was the forgotten man as Swindon Town went on to play in the semi-finals of the League Cup.

By this time I had recovered from my ankle injury and was starting to settle down in Swindon. In November the Club had two defeats in a row after a wonderful cup run and very good league form.

At Coventry City I met up again with Joe Mercer who was in the stand watching our League Cup match. Joe always the gentleman had kept a watch on what was happening to me after Manchester City and he knew I was finding it a struggle at Swindon. All he said was, "Chris, enjoy being out on the field playing football and play with a smile on your face. These will be the best moments in your life to be a professional footballer." I took Joe's words away with me and slowly my luck changed for the better at Swindon.

I suddenly found myself in the team for an FA Cup match at Grantham.

Strange place to go: we were on a hiding to nothing on a ground which was open on two sides and any Saturday afternoon shoppers could watch. With a League Cup semi-final play-off due after we had played Burnley home and away, I thought this was my chance to force my way into the team.

They didn't manage to beat us and in front of 4,000 fans I opened my goal scoring account for Swindon Town with a late goal. It was swiftly followed by a second from John Smith and we won 2-0. I silently thanked Joe Mercer for the fatherly advice. Our paths never crossed again and he was not at the Hotel in Manchester just prior to the League Cup final when I met up with some of my old friends from Manchester City.

The following week we played Brighton and Hove Albion in the League but I found myself disconsolately out of the side again. Danny Williams had gone back to the exact side that had fought through to being one game away from Wembley and a League Cup Final; Don Rogers scored that day in a 1-0 win and in December Swindon Town made it to Wembley, beating Burnley 3-2 after extra time at West Bromwich Albion.

In our dressing room after the game, Danny Williams jubilantly said that the 12 men on duty that day would play at Wembley in March. It was an expansive gesture three months before the actual day of the Cup Final, as a lot could happen in that time. Over Christmas the team managed to keep up its form although we were drawing quite a few games. In those days of one point for a draw and two for a win, a lot of sides were vying for promotion.

John Smith, who was a stocky player, suddenly developed a hamstring problem and our left-back Owen Dawson a serious groin injury, both of which lingered into March 1969.

Meanwhile my form was returning and the euphoria of reaching Wembley and being high up in the League table had softened the fans dislike for me. I was getting a run in the team in place of John Smith and John Trollope had taken over at left-back for Owen Dawson. By the middle of January I had established myself in the team. Saturday 18th January 1969 we drew 0-0 at the county ground against Luton in front of the 'Match of the Day' cameras and on the 24th January opened my League account with two goals in a 5-3 win at Tranmere Rovers. I only wished that my goal scoring had been at the County Ground to show the fans what I could do.

But they didn't have to wait long as four days later we beat Oldham Athletic in front of 21,000 fans 5-1. I got a hat-trick, two from close range but for the third I had to beat a defender and crash the ball into the net from 20 yards. Frank Burrows and Roger Smart scored the other two goals that night.

I had turned the fans round and they applauded me off the field. This gave Danny Williams a problem for the League Cup final if Smith or Dawson became fit in the next month. We were flying in the league and went seven games without defeat.

Wembley was getting closer and Danny Williams, having pronounced that the semi-final line-up would play at Wembley, suddenly struck the rocks as neither John Smith nor Owen Dawson looked like being fit.

John Trollope's form and my goal scoring had created what would be to most managers today a "nice" problem but Williams, with whom I did not get on, was looking for an excuse to get me out of the side if either injured player looked like returning.

Ten days before Wembley we went to Gillingham and lost 2-0. Williams took the first chance he had to substitute me, even though I was the most likely to score on that day. Willie Penman, who was substitute in the semi-final, took my place and stayed in the side the following week at Stockport County. I became substitute for that game and was in the same Hotel in Manchester as my mates from Manchester City.

The Manchester *Football Pink* had an article on me leaving Manchester City and looking good for a Cup Final spot the following week at Wembley. Alan Oakes and Glyn Pardoe were saying well done, and good luck for next week. I said hopefully I would play but had the spectre of John Smith looming over my shoulder. He hadn't played in a long time but it was rumoured he might try his leg out in a reserve game at Birmingham City, three days before Wembley.

We lost 2-1 at Stockport County and the Manager did not put me on during the game which was ominous for my chances the following week. Seventy-two hours before the final against Arsenal, the news I dreaded was relayed to me. What a surprise: John Smith had pronounced himself fit having played half a match in which he never moved more than 20 yards either side of the half way line on the right wing.

Danny Williams went with this risky strategy taking a chance with his fitness on what was going to be a mud-bath of a pitch (following the Horse of the Year Show). And it was rumoured that at least half of the Arsenal side had been down with a bug the week prior to Wembley.

All Danny said was: "Sorry Chris, I was always going with the team that played in the semi-final, however if John shows any reaction you will play."

Well, John stayed fit but the unfortunate Owen Dawson lost out and John Trollope played in the final. In the days of only one substitute I became the unlucky thirteenth man at Wembley.

When the only chance to play at Wembley if you weren't an International was in an FA or League Cup Final, Williams' words were like a body blow.

My wife to be Therese was coming over for the game. I cancelled the air tickets from Malta and gave all my Wembley tickets away to friends in Swindon. I had to endure the bus trip to Wembley, Wembley Way, walking out of the Wembley dressing room after the twelve players and suffer the reception after we had won, besides the open bus tour round Swindon on the Sunday afternoon. It was the greatest day in Swindon Town's footballing history at the time but the blackest day in my footballing career. "Grin and bear it", they always say and that I had to do over a long weekend. Anybody who thinks that you are "happy for the team" and a good "team player" is a long way from the truth in these situations. I was a professional who wanted the chance to play in a Wembley final and felt that it had been taken away from me by a manager who made a lucky call on the day and had an inspired player in Don Rogers at his best.

I know it is churlish, but the tankard which all the players of the winning team won stands on my mantelpiece and I keep my pens in it.

John Smith, by the way, survived 60 minutes before being replaced by Willie Penman and only played a handful of games to the end of the season with that ham-string problem.

The question for the reader is, "In the days of one substitute and such an important day in a Club's history, would you have gambled with an injured player on a heavy pitch?". Williams did and got lucky.

Meanwhile I had harsh words with Williams over taking a risk with a long-term injured player which put me on the side lines until two games before the end of the season.

To say that dislike had turned to hate was the understatement. He wasn't a good manager, but in Swindon history he will go down as one of its most successful if luckiest of managers.

Swindon still looked like promotion candidates but with two games left definitely needed a point in the penultimate game of the season at Rotherham. It finally looked as if Williams luck with the team had run out.

Nobody needed to say that the tension was getting to the players and it was evident in their play. We had an injury on the way to Rotherham and I had become the Manager's reluctant substitute.

With ten minutes left we were losing 1-0 after Storrie of Rotherham had swept the ball home in the 51st minute. We never looked like scoring, and the team was struggling to put any passes together never mind create a chance on the Rotherham goal.

Danny Williams seemed at a loss over the situation. He never looked at me but said, "Well I suppose I will have to put you on then."

I looked malevolently back at him and said, "Don't do me any favours will you?"

112

Without a warm-up I was onto the pitch. I had no qualms about the game as I hadn't been part of the side since before Wembley and was really playing for myself and a move away in the close-season.

Stan Harland blasted a ball down field in my general direction and I spun off the centre half and found myself through a square defence and running in on goal. Jim Furnell was the Rotherham goalkeeper. He came out to narrow the angle and I slipped it past him for the equaliser. This gave us the point we needed to secure promotion. It was total irony that Williams had to turn to me to ensure promotion and a malevolent pleasure in my case.

The Press came in and asked Williams if he would have a photo with Chris Jones and the boot that scored the all important goal. He declined and I, smiling, just waved my right boot at him.

The headlines in the papers were *Clincher, Jones takes Swindon Up*. It must have been particularly galling for Danny Williams to accept that I had secured the valuable point

Of course the team had plenty of heroes during that campaign but in a way it was just a minor triumph for me in such a traumatic year in my footballing career.

We won our last game of the season and would play the next season in the Second Division. Swindon Town had been out of the Second Division for four years and the crowd were delirious with us in gaining promotion.

Maybe that was just a rehearsal for what would transpire five years later at York in 1974.

In June 1969 I went back to Malta and was married to Therese In St Julian's Church in St Julian's, Silema. We had the reception by the Plevna Hotel poolside and it was a lavish affair. While relaxing in Malta on honeymoon I jubilantly heard the word that Danny Williams was leaving to manage Sheffield Wednesday.

A week before I had heard he had been offered a new three year contract at Swindon and suddenly he had resigned and become Manager of Sheffield Wednesday.

This could change all my plans as a new manager could mean a new beginning. I had managed to win over most of my doubters of the previous season and thought that Therese and I might stay and see who the new Manager was.

At this time I had not bought a house in Swindon but had arranged to stay with our very good friends Kate and Frank Strange. Sadly, both have passed away now but we still have very pleasant memories of our time there.

Pre-season brought a new Manager in Fred Ford, just as we were preparing for the Anglo-Italian League Cup against Roma. Fred managed the Club until November 1971. By then Dave Mackay had joined as a player with a view to him taking on the Manager's job. To his credit Dave would not usurp Fred Ford as Manager but the inevitable happened in November of 1971 when he was dismissed.

1969 also brought a new centre forward in Arthur Horsfield from Middlesbrough whom I had played against in a Youth team match at Maine Road five years earlier when I scored a memorable hat-trick.

SWINDON TOWN 1969-1970

And so I found myself battling Peter Noble and Arthur Horsfield for the striking roles. It looked like I was going to be in the position of super sub again, and that is how it turned out.

However, the difference this season was that the crowd had taken to me and Therese and I had many good friends in Swindon. We rented a house on the Nythe Estate next to Frank Burrows and his wife Mary. For this season at least I was going to fight for a place in the Second Division team.

As it was to turn out, Noble and Horsfield kept scoring and this reduced my starting appearances. Most of the time, Fred Ford always encouraged me during that season.

We were to play Roma in a new Cup called the Anglo-Italian League Cup Winners' Cup. This was to reward Swindon for winning the League Cup but not being allowed to enter the Fairs Cup (now the UEFA Cup or the Europa League) competition as we were in the Third Division at the time.

The Coppa Italia winners were AS Roma, and we were to play them over two legs in August and early September 1969.

The Manager of AS Roma was Helenio Herrera and he had Fabio Capello as a midfield player from 1967-1970. In 1968 they finished eighth in the Italian League and the Coppa Italia was his first major trophy. Also in the Roma side were three Internationals, Ronato Cappellini, Liano Spinosi (19 caps for Italy) and Alberto Ginulfi, their goalkeeper.

We went to Rome for the first leg, which was played in the Stadio Olimpico on the 27th August 1969 and came away with a creditable 2-1 defeat. Amid the terrific din of fireworks, bugles and klaxons horns we put in a really top class performance

It was mainly a defensive game for us and we nearly got to half time 0-0. However they were given a penalty when Elvio Salvori was supposedly upended by Roger Smart. Fifty-five thousand fans minus our 100 supporters couldn't be wrong, could they? Fabio Enzo converted and the fanatical Roma supporters set off fireworks into the air.

I came on at half time and was immediately made welcome to Italian tackling when Fabio Capello scythed through me. No free kick. We managed to break out of defence a few times in the second half. On one of these Peter Noble chipped the ball over the Roma Goalkeeper Alberto Ginulfi's head and into the net to make it 1-1. Again the fireworks went off into the night sky: what a great atmosphere in which to play football.

It was all hands to the pumps after that as we had 11 men behind the ball. From a cross from Peiro, Roma got the winner when Ronato Cappellini got above Frank Burrows and headed into the net. The noise from the fireworks horns and bugles was deafening to the end, although we made the better chances in the last 15 minutes.

We held on to the final whistle amidst the bedlam and the fireworks and were confident that we could reverse the result at the County Ground.

In September 1969 we played the second leg and Fabio Capello was again in the side. We brought the scores level within 15 minutes through Arthur Horsfield, who went on to complete his hat-trick in the second half. Don Rogers got our other goal as Roma capitulated and we went on to pick up the second trophy of 1969. Halcyon footballing days for Swindon Town, and a deserved medal for me, unlike the tankard from the League Cup final in which I didn't participate. Sadly the medals would be stolen in 2012 along with the Anglo-Italian inter-leagues medal which followed shortly afterwards.

The Italian FA was so impressed with the event they went about organising this next Anglo-Italian competition for the same season.

We reached the final by winning our group, which involved playing Juventus and Napoli home and away. We played Juventus and Napoli at the County Ground beating Juventus 4-0 and losing to Napoli 1-0.

On the return fixtures we beat Juventus in Turin 1-0 with Peter Noble scoring. It was a really rough game with one player going over the top on me and I was only just able to limp out the game. We beat Napoli 1-0 and advanced to the Final as we got points for goals scored.

In the final where we were again up against Napoli whom we had defeated the week before. In their ranks was Altafini, a prolific goal scorer who had played both for Brazil and Italy at International level.

The game was marred by mob violence when the crowd, upset with the Napoli team losing 3-0, started to tear up the concrete strips on the seats in the stands and hurl them at the players. They then started to invade the field.

The *Daily Mail* reported it as one of the worst riots in soccer history, causing £20,000 of damage (a huge sum at the time) and leaving at least 40 people injured. Luckily none of our fans were involved or injured but we were left cowering on the far side of the pitch while the riot police tried to restore order. Paul Schiller the Austrian referee had no alternative but to abandon the game. The Cup was presented to us in the most ludicrous of circumstances. The game had been announced as abandoned and the Cup presented to Swindon while concrete was still being hurled on to the pitch.

Fred Ford suggested we try and pacify the 55,000 crowd by doing a lap of honour with the Cup. Even with a 12ft deep safety ditch around the ground this was a dangerous venture and only Stan Harland and Fred Ford made a move – but were soon sent back as beer cans, cardboard cushions, rocks and abuse were hurled at them.

It took us 15 minutes of sheltering on the far side of the field before we were given a safety gauntlet by the Italian riot police to get us down into the dressing rooms. In the dressing room we could still hear the racket above and concrete dust settled all over us as it permeated the changing area. We heard later that the Neapolitan fans had set fire to the cushions and gone on to a senseless orgy of vandalism and violence, which left several police injured.

The official reception at the Hotel Napoli was cancelled and it was over an hour before we could board the coach with a protective guard of riot police to manoeuvre us away from the stadium. We were told to put our cases up against the windows as we moved away from the ground in case of flying concrete smashing the windows. In the street we could see the police engaged in running fights with hooligans.

I didn't go back with the Swindon team to the UK as I was heading to Malta to meet up with Therese and have our usual holiday.

At the airport I met up with Gigi Peronace, who was the agent for many English footballers going to play in Italy, and an instigator of the Anglo-Italian games. He told me he hoped the inaugural matches would not be the last but was ashamed with the way the final had ended and of the Napoli supporters involved.

Gigi told me of all the transfers he had been negotiating including Alex Stock to AS Roma in 1957. In that year he also negotiated the transfer of John Charles from Leeds United to Juventus for £65,000 and a £10,000 signing-on fee.

I was later privileged to play with the Leeds United Former Players' Association in charity games and got to know John Charles very well. He was always the gentleman and many were the times he had a kind word for my Uncle Bill at these games.

He used to joke with me that I was on a game to game contract with the team, being an outsider and not having played for Leeds United. On a serious note he did say that I should have played right back and not centre forward as I could maybe have earned a few International call-ups in that position – quite a compliment from the Great Man.

Gigi, at the time when White and Swales were making their first venture into football with Altrincham, was in 1961 negotiating the transfer of Jimmy Greaves from Chelsea to AC Milan and two players to Torino. They were Denis Law from Manchester City and Joe Baker from Hibernian.

Gigi, with pride, told me of his friend Matt Busby and his part in transferring Denis back to Manchester, this time to United in 1962. Gigi came to live in London and bought a home in Twickenham.

He was the General Manager for the Italian National side in 1978 at the World Cup and did the same job in the European Championship in 1980. Sadly this wonderful little man suffered a fatal heart attack in Montivideo and died in the Italian Team Manager Enzo Bearzot's arms in December 1980.

It was only in Swindon and Naples that I got to know him, but he loved the English and the English players in the Anglo-Italian tournament. I really got on well with him.

Back in League action, Swindon were going really well by the end of October 1969. Peter Noble was injured in mid-August and I made a start against high flying Cardiff City at the County Ground. In I came, had a good match and scored the two goals that defeated Cardiff City 2-1.

This posed a problem for Fred Ford as Peter was going to be fit for the Saturday match at Aston Villa. Two goals usually means that you would hold your place in the team but when Saturday came I was back on the bench and the team backed up the Manager's choice by winning 2-0 and going on the following week to thrash Charlton Athletic 5-0 and beat Swansea in the League Cup 3-2.

My great game against Cardiff City was nearly forgotten in the barrage of goals the attack was scoring and it was November before I got a start again.

This time it was Don Rogers out on the side-lines and we played with three strikers for the first time against Norwich City. They were always a good side for me to play against and the goalkeeper Kevin Keelan in particular must have hated seeing my name on the team sheet.

I remember the game for both good and now humorous events although at the time the game may have turned pear-shaped for me.

As I have said Fred Ford was a good Manager for me and although I felt he should have picked me more often, I could not argue with the number of goals our prolific attack was scoring. After three months of the season we looked like we could get promotion to the First Division.

In training I had been working hard and kept trying to catch the eye with my ability. I always felt that I could make a crossfield pass of about 50 yards. I kept trying it in training until finally I managed to land one right on Don Roger's foot. After training Fred fettled me and in no uncertain terms told me not to try it in a game.

"You," he said in his great booming voice, "only need to hold the ball up, lay it off and get back in the box where you are at your best. Leave the creative stuff to Donald and the midfield, OK?"

I said, "Fine, Boss," thinking I can still make this pass in a match.

Roger Smart used to take the micky out of Fred due to him having a forefinger missing. Roger used to put up his hand with his forefinger hidden and say: "Five pints Boss please." How he got away with it I don't know as I am sure he would have murdered anybody else (except Don Rogers, of course).

I believe that Fred lost the finger in an accident with a hand grenade in the war.

Well, Don was injured and I was selected for the game against Norwich City. It was a poor first half in front of nearly 20,000 fans and the game was going to be a stalemate.

However, Joe Butler and John Trollope managed to create a chance for Peter Noble to score and with five minutes left I received a pass from Joe Butler on the edge of the box, controlled it, turned, and scored with a low shot from the edge of the box past Kevin Keelan's despairing dive.. We were 2-0 up, the fans were delirious and I was looking for my second goal.

Moments later, Peter Downsborough, our goalkeeper, had the ball in his hands and I had pulled wide to the right and called for it. He threw it out and just next to the dugout I controlled the ball and realised that the crossfield pass to Don Heath was on and that John Trollope was on the overlap. Two Swindon players against the full back looked a fair gamble.

The alarm bells did not ring but as I drew back my foot to make the pass a booming voice shouted "YOU, NO, you prat Jones!"

Too late. The ball was on its way and it looked great in the air until the full back popped up between the two Swindon players, intercepted the pass and was off down the right wing. I didn't wait, and with the voice bellowing "You Bastard Jones" I raced off on a fast diagonal to try and intercept the defender. I just made it and slid the ball out for a corner.

That voice was still shouting "You..." over and over and it seemed to be getting louder. Daft like, I asked John Trollope who Fred was shouting at, knowing quite well it was me.

"You, you fricking idiot, who do you think he's shouting at?"

"He sounds loud, where is he?" said I without looking round.

John said, "He is running along the touchline shaking his fist and you can hear him shouting, can't you?" No technical area in those days, but I wished there had been on this occasion.

The referee hadn't allowed the corner to be taken and I said to John, "Where is he now?" Fred was still shouting.

"YOUUUU bastard Jones."

"He has been stopped by the linesman on the 18-yard box" said John with a chuckle.

"Thank God for that," said I as the Norwich crowd behind the goal took up the chant, "You bastard Jones..." They didn't have much else to chant about on that day.

I managed to clear the ball at the near post for a throw-in and followed it out to the left wing. I finished the game on that wing, as far from the dugout as possible and sent Don Heath over to play on the right wing.

I believe if Fred had got closer on that day with that grenade in his hand he would have chucked it at me. I really needed a hole in the ground and even winning 2-0 I still had to face him in the dressing room afterwards. I loitered behind on the pitch at the final whistle but finally had to go in and face the music.

"YOU! Lucky we won! But you are back for extra training tomorrow."

"But it's Sunday Boss and we go to Church on Sunday," said I, lying through my teeth.

"Be here, otherwise the next time you are in Church will be when we read over you." I dutifully turned up the next day for extra training and vowed not to try that crossfield pass again, at least not while Fred Ford was the Manager.

At that point in the season we were sixth in the Second Division. Don Rogers was fit for the next game and automatically back in the team and yours truly ended up back on the bench.

However I was returned to the side in late November at the County Ground against Huddersfield Town. We won 2-1 and I scored the winner in the last minute. There was no comeback for the then Second Division leaders.

1970 started with a 4-0 win in the Third Round of the FA Cup against Blackburn Rovers away and we were drawn against Chester in the fourth round.

I was back in the team for that game which we won 4-2 and again I was on the score sheet. In front of 22,000 supporters Arthur Horsfield got a couple of goals and Roger Smart and I the other two.

We went on to beat Scunthorpe United in the Fifth Round and were drawn against Leeds United in the quarter-final at the County Ground.

We honestly fancied our chances against what was one of the best sides in the Country at the time. We thought we would get them in the mud and out-fight them.

However Don Revie's team were battle hardened and streetwise and knew what to expect. They had two very good strikers in Mick Jones and Allan Clarke and with Jack Charlton, Norman Hunter, Peter Lorimer and Billy Bremner in the side it was a battle royal. Unfortunately we came out of the match losing 2-0 in front of a near record crowd of 27,500.

It took Leeds United three games to get past Manchester United in the semi-final, two 0-0 draws and eventually a 1-0 win. In the final against Chelsea they drew 2-2 at Wembley and lost the replay 2-1 at Old Trafford. The scoring frustrations under Danny Williams were just distant memories, although I was still having to battle against two in-form strikers for the starting berth in the team.

SWINDON TOWN 1970-1971

After two good years of success, the second season under Fred Ford was a disappointment for me. Again I had to compete with Arthur Horsfield and Peter Noble for a centre forward position and I was the third preferred choice once again. It would not be until after Christmas before I got into the starting eleven. We were again going to finish in mid-table, losing three matches all season at the County Ground but winning only three away from home.

In the League Cup we had beaten Liverpool 2-0 at the County Ground in the third round but went out to Fulham at Craven Cottage 1-0 in October of 1970. I had again made fleeting appearances from the subs' bench' but had not managed to score.

In early January our interest in the FA Cup fell by the wayside. We had beaten QPR at Loftus Road 2-1 before coming a cropper in late January 4-0 at Leeds United. It was a workmanlike season for me as a professional, an important member of the squad but not regularly starting games and I was getting restive and thinking of a move North to another club.

However 1971 was a highlight year in mine and Therese's life with the birth of our first daughter, Sheriden, on St Patrick's Day, 17th March. We had two daughters, Francesca being born in York in 1984.

However Sheriden's birth coincided with our move into a club house on the Nythe Estate in Swindon and the Club offering me an extension to my contract which I had accepted.

By coincidence as we celebrated Sheriden's birth I suddenly got a run in the first team. During March and April 1971 I was to score three important goals against Blackburn Rovers, Charlton Athletic and Luton Town.

Fred Ford was under pressure in early March, as the team had lost four games on the trot. I liked to think I helped to keep the Manager in a job with my goals and we finished the season in what was finally a respectable 12th position in the League.

Fred's position was put under severe pressure when the Board paid a record fee of £20,000 for Dave Mackay from Derby County with a view to him becoming Player-Manager in April 1971. The idea was for Fred to move to Chief Scout and Dave to take over as Manager straight away.

Dave Mackay had a long and distinguished playing career and had been part of the Tottenham Hotspur's Double-winning team of 1961. In 1969 he shared the Football Writers' Association Footballer of the Year Award jointly with my old captain Tony Book of Manchester City. At this time he was playing for Brian Clough at Derby County in a sweeper role and used his influence and experience to play a counter-attacking game and so gain promotion to the First Division.

Dave declined to take the Manager's job and Fred continued as Manager for the rest of the campaign.

As in the previous year the season was extended because of our involvement in the Anglo-Italian Cup. Our season had ended in the League on the 1st May 1971 when I scored the equalising goal at Luton Town, away.

We then had three weeks to wait before finally playing Bologna at the County Ground, drawing 2-2, and three days later playing Sampdoria and winning 4-1. I didn't score in either game and the games were poorly supported.

We flew to Bologna and lost 3-1 in front of 25,000 fans and then, virtually out of the Cup, travelled to Sampdoria in Genoa and beat them 2-1 in front of the Italian and English television cameras. This game only attracted just over 2,000 fans and we relinquished the Cup which we had won the year before in Naples. However it was always a great experience to play against clubs from other countries and test your ability against the best sides in Europe at that time.

Bologna went on to play in the final that year but lost to Blackpool 2-1.

SWINDON TOWN 1971-1972

After two reasonable years of success under Fred Ford in the Second Division the third was going to become a disappointment for Swindon. At the start of the season Fred Ford again decided on the Peter Noble-Arthur Horsfield combination in attack and I was left kicking my heels on the bench. Fred was obviously still under pressure from the presence of Dave Mackay and the added problem of where to play Stan Harland or leave him out of the starting line-up. Fred tried to solve the problem by playing Stan in midfield but that was like putting a square peg into a round hole and was doomed to failure.

This move was to try and appease the Board who respected Stan for what he had done for the Club over the past years. However Stan lost the captaincy to Dave Mackay and was sold to Birmingham City for £15,000 shortly afterwards.

The season started badly and we lost the first game 4-1 at Blackpool, the second against Charlton Athletic at home before drawing 0-0 at Carlisle. The fans were restless and Fred under pressure put me in the starting line-up.

We drew the next two games at Watford and QPR and I was then back on the subs' bench for our trip to Sunderland where we lost 1-0. By the end of September the results were only average and we were languishing in mid-table, four points above the relegation zone.

I was getting on quite well with Dave Mackay as he tried to motivate the side as they went through a bad period, with players losing confidence and goals having dried up.

I was back in the team on 17th September playing against Fulham at the County Ground. Fulham was always a lucky Club for me and I duly notched a goal as we struck form and Don Rogers, Peter Noble and Joe Butler brought us a 4-0 victory.

For the time being Fred Ford's job was safe and the following week we went to Cardiff City and beat them 1-0 and I scored the only goal in front of 16,000 fans. It was one of my best goals ever, on the volley with my right foot from the edge of the penalty area. It crashed in off the underside of the bar and I raced away to the halfway line to celebrate. Dave Mackay wanted to congratulate me and, puffing, grabbed me to slow me down, saying in his Scottish burr, "Slow down son, great goal, but don't waste your energy." Wise man, was Dave, who had seen it all before and realised the game had not yet been won.

I held my place in the team through October but our run of results petered away as we lost at Hull City. In their ranks was Ian Butler who was supplying Ken Wagstaffe and Chris Chilton with all the chances they were converting. Oh! To have this guy in our team, I thought at the time. We obviously had Don Rogers on the wing but he usually cut in to shoot himself and strikers picked up the scraps if he failed to score.

We then lost 2-0 at home against Bristol City in front of a nearly 24,000 Derby crowd. We played through October and Fred Ford's position as Manager was becoming untenable. Of the next three games we won one, lost one, and drew another before losing to Sheffield Wednesday away 1-0 and Middlesbrough at home 3-0 at the end of the month.

Fred lost his job at the beginning of November 1971 and Dave Mackay took over as Manager. Fred subsequently spent a number of years as Chief Scout and Youth team Coach at Oxford United where he brought through a conveyor belt of young talent in the 70s.

I was again out of the team for the next two games but after a 2-0 home defeat to Milwall I was selected by Dave against Preston North End at home. We drew 1-1 and then went to Burnley the following week and in front of the *Match of the Day* cameras won 2-1.

Peter Noble got the first with a header from a cross from the left wing from Joe Butler and I pounced on a fumble by Jeff Parton, the Burnley goalkeeper, from a shot by Don Rogers and slid it into the corner of the net for the winner just before half-time.

The ground was open on one side at the time, as the Bob Lord stand was being built. I believe they sold Martin Dobson to pay for it. That was to be my last goal for Swindon Town and the game the following week against Norwich City (the League leaders at the time) was to be my last for the Club, on 4th December 1971.

Unfortunately we lost that match 1-0 and Dave Mackay reverted to Noble and Horsfield as the strike partnership.

At the end of the month, Dave had said that Oldham Athletic, managed by Jimmy Frizzell, would like to take me on loan and that it was a good chance to get some first team football. It was not much of a subtle hint from Dave that my time was up at Swindon Town: he was trying to recoup some money for his own signings.

Fed up with being in and out of the team and Peter Noble and Arthur Horsfield being preferred to me in the starting line-up, I said I would consider it. I was actually elated as I felt the North of England was where I wanted to be and that there were more clubs to choose from than down in the South West.

I talked it over with Therese and then with Uncle Bill in Altrincham. The result was that I moved back home to Altrincham with my family for the loan spell, thankful that Jimmy Frizzell was interested in me forming a strike partnership with their prolific goal scorer David Shaw.

As it was a loan move I expected to be back in Swindon, if only for a short while. The Club house on the Nythe Estate was still full of our furniture, but closed for our return in the near future.

While I was away in January 1972 the County Ground attendance record was broken as Arsenal came to Swindon Town to play in the FA Cup. 32,000 fans crammed in to see the game which Arsenal won 2-0.

It seemed after I left that the Club started to slowly deteriorate and would finish the season in 11th position. At the time the Swindon Town Board were getting into dire financial straits. As the year progressed Arthur Horsfield would be sold to Charlton Athletic in June and the whole playing staff was put on the transfer list in October to help fund the building of the North Stand. Two months into the 1972-73 campaign the unthinkable happened: Swindon Town's icon Don Rogers was sold to Crystal Palace for £147,000. The Club at the time were two points off the relegation zone. To replace Don, Dave Mackay bought Tommy Jenkins from Southampton for £60,000 and then promptly resigned saying he was going to manage Nottingham Forest. I was away from the Club at this time but sad to see them finish 16th in the Second Division and the following season slump into the Third Division just as York City moved into the Second Division. We passed each other like ships in the night.

In 1971 we'd had a new beginning with the birth of Sheriden in Swindon and as the year ended I hoped for success at a club further North. Would Oldham fulfil that dream? Maybe so, but as it turned out in a most unexpected way.

We lived back in Hamon Road, Altrincham with Bill and Hazel and I travelled up to Oldham Athletic daily and thought I might move back to my roots here near the City of Manchester.

I played three games for Oldham Athletic that month along with Harry Dowd who had joined from Manchester City, and scored a goal at Mansfield in a 1-1 draw. I would by the end of my career have scored for every club I played for, which at the time was a record in the *Guinness Book of Football*.

We went to RAF Valley in the third week of my loan for a change of scene in training. On the second day there Jimmy Frizzell called me over and said that Dave McKay wanted to talk to me on the telephone urgently. Jimmy would not say what it was about but I gathered it would be something to do with my career.

So it was to be, as I rang Dave and was told that Walsall had made an offer for me. I saw Jimmy Frizzel outside and, really wanting to stay at Oldham Athletic, asked him about buying me. Jimmy said, "Sorry Chris, we haven't the sort of money I heard that Walsall were willing to pay for you." I liked Jimmy Frizzel and said, "Thanks Jimmy, I wish you and all the players good luck at Oldham except when you play any side I am in." We parted in good humour but our paths were destined to cross a few years down the line.

I signed for Walsall in February 1972 and played out most of the season while I travelled from Altrincham daily, training in the morning and house-searching with the help of the Walsall Secretary in the afternoon. It was quite a tiring experience but we managed to find a very nice house on Birmingham Road which backed on to the West Midlands College of Further Education about a mile from Fellows Park. It had an open aspect and would be worth a fortune in today's market. I brought Therese down to see the house with Sheriden and she loved it.

We never went back to Swindon. Our furniture was delivered and we settled in, hoping for a long stay. However, it would only be a year before we were on the move again and this time back to a City, though not Manchester as I had hoped. My time at Walsall was successful and I managed in a season and a half to score 14 League goals in 59 appearances which wasn't bad considering the clashes I had with John Smith and Stan Bennett.

A TALE OF TWO CITIES

A fabula duorum

YORK 1973-1974

It was the summer of 1973 when we first came to York. Therese and Sheriden and me were given a guided tour of York by Tom Johnston, the Manager of York City.

We got the impression that it might be a good club to come to. However, I was doing well at Walsall, having finished the season with a good ratio of goals to games and was the Club's leading scorer with 12 goals and looking forward to another goal scoring season with my new striking partner Bobby Shinton.

We had a large detached house in Birmingham Road, Walsall and were settled in after half a season of travelling to training from Manchester where we were living with my Uncle Bill and Aunt Hazel.

My car knew the M6 well by the time we found and moved into the house and to suddenly be asked to talk to York City became an awkward decision.

However Walsall was in a state of turbulence at the time and I had three Managers in my short time at the Club. They were Bill Moore who signed me from Swindon Town, John Smith whom I played with at Swindon and took over in October 1972 and caretaker Boss Jimmy McEwan who was in charge from March to June 1973.

By the time Ronnie Allen took over in June I was already on my way to York City. The Walsall Chairman was Ken Wheldon who in 1972 took over the Club and rescued it from financial oblivion. It was he who negotiated my move from Walsall to York with Tom Johnston and York City Secretary George Teasdale.

People were telling me that York was a wonderful city to live in and that if I came I probably would not want to leave. I scoffed at this at the time as Derek Kevan, a player whom I knew at Manchester City said, "Chris, as a goal scorer you will be liked for a few years and then things become a matter of fact with the fans and it is best to move on." I always remembered that and thought that York would be just another club in a striker's career.

We went back to Walsall after that short visit in a quandary as to what to do. We had just settled comfortably in on Birmingham Road in Walsall after living out of a suitcase for the first two years of Sheriden's life.

Against that, the last season at Walsall, although successful, had been a bit traumatic. John Smith, who I had been with at Swindon, was in charge with Bill Moore at Walsall and we had an altercation in the dressing room at Brentford when we went a goal down on the stroke of half-time. John tore into the team, me included and I lost it, tearing my boot off and throwing it at him. I missed, which prompted Smithy to say, "You couldn't hit me from three feet – you have no fucking chance of scoring in this game," and subbed me.

I spent the next three weeks with the reserves before going back into the side. However, during that duration I had another altercation, this time with Stan Bennett, our centre half, in a practice match. Stan back-elbowed me in the mouth, breaking one of my teeth, and I went after him and chinned him. A big lad, Stan: he flung one at me and a brawl ensued.

I asked John Smith, " What are you going to do about Bennett breaking my teeth and cutting my eye open?"

"Nothing," he said so I walked off to find a dentist and a doctor.

Nowadays it would be classed as an assault, but in those days we got on with it. Stan Bennett and I played in the same team until the end of the season but the animosity was still there.

So, decision time: I had an appointment with Mr Wheldon. I said I was reticent about the move and had told Tom Johnston that I was not sure I would sign for York City.

The Chairman said, "I think it is best that you make the move as we have to pay summer wages and it's a long close season before we get any real income into the Club. The offer on the table of £10,000 would go a long way to keeping the Club in a viable state."

He went on to say, "Some of the wages might not get paid on time, including yours." It flashed through my mind wickedly that Stan Bennett and John Smith would not get paid either.

He said that they might also sell Bobby Shinton (who later went to Norwich City) but he thought it was best for me to go to York City. I said, "Well, I can't go for just ten per cent of the transfer fee, out of that £500 had to go into the Professional Footballers' Graduation Fund and out of the £500 left about £130 would go in tax leaving me with about £370," I said. "I won't move for that amount of money."

The Chairman asked if Therese and I liked York. I reticently said, "Yes it looks reasonable and the team seem solid defensively and they should have a good season if they can score goals."

I already had first-hand knowledge of York City's defence as we had played them on 24th March 1973 at Fellows Park when we were both in danger of relegation to the Fourth Division. With six games to go Walsall needed a point to be sure of survival and York City were in mid- table. However they only managed two wins in their last 13 matches and would find themselves needing to win their last game of the season 2-1 at Rotherham to stay up on goal average

However the game at Fellows Park was a strange affair as I had four good chances to score and was foiled by two outstanding saves by their Goalkeeper Graeme Crawford.

The headline in *The Argos* the following day was *Jones the Miss* and looking at the cutting I don't know whether they were relating to my gender, lack of goal-scoring ability or both.

Those two great saves put me off the other two chances I had, heading one over the bar and the other past the post.

My other lasting impression besides the 0-0 draw was what a tough afternoon I had against their back four. I knew Phil Burrows from our Youth team games at Manchester City eight years earlier but this was a different Phil, very confident and mature with seven years' hardened league experience behind him.

However I thought I could take him on as he was all left foot, so come inside him and head for goal. Wrong! Phil might have passed with his left foot but he couldn't half tackle with both feet and proved it. No friendship there.

My striking partner Bobby Shinton didn't like the look of York's defence and decided to play two-touch about ten yards deeper than the action while all the time saying, "Well played Jonesy and great battling," as I pulled myself up off the ground from yet another scything tackle.

I looked up to see who had hammered me and there was Barry Swallow saying, "Great tackle, send him over here if he gets up and I will have a piece of him." Then another player piped up and said, "If he comes over here he will get even worse treatment." That turned out to be John Mackin and I thought what a vicious bunch of thugs York had for a defence.

Bobby Shinton had read it well. Bobby was bearded, but didn't get away from being derided by York as they dished out the verbals. "Send Jesus over here and I'll crucify him," said Mackin. Not a very Christian bunch, York City's back four'.

These thoughts all went through my mind when coming to a decision on joining York. Which defence would I like to have at my back as a centre forward?

The only answer to that was York City's – goalkeeper Graeme Crawford and that back four of Mackin (later Stone), Swallow, Topping and Burrows. They reminded me of the Swindon Town defence whom I played with in our promotion push from the Third Division to the Second in 1969 and League Cup run to the final at Wembley and they also gave very little away.

That was Peter Downsbrough in goal with Rod Thomas, Stan Harland, Frank Burrows (no relation to Phil other than in tackling) and John Trollope.

Realising that a move seemed inevitable I asked, "What could you offer me financially if I was willing to go?"

"If you go, we will pay all your removal fees, help to sell your house in Walsall and on a gentleman's agreement and my word of honour will give you £1,500 net when Walsall come up to play York during the season."

A trustworthy soul was I, and I replied, "That would be OK, but if the first game is at Walsall I wanted paying then, otherwise I might have to wait until after Christmas for the payment."

That was agreed and he told me they desperately needed me to go, although he wasn't trying to push me out of the door. It was purely down to finances. When I look back I wonder if I wasn't being kidded out of the door. Anyway I agreed to go back up to York to talk with Tom Johnston.

A canny man, was Tom. I found he had watched me a few times over the past months and he knew how to slip in the missing pieces of his team jig-saw to create a quality side.

The last words from the Walsall Chairman were, "Chris, take the forms with you and if things seem favourable to you with Tom Johnston and George Teasdale you could sign straight away for York City."

I collected the forms and am sure he gave me a farewell wave as I went to pick up Therese and Sheriden at the house in Altrincham and head further North. I could not dream how fortuitous that trip was going to be.

The result was that I met up with Tom Johnston who gave me a tour of the Woodthorpe Estate and showed Therese and me the Club house at 46 Moorcroft Road where we would live. It was the house Paul Aimson had lived in.

Paul, who Tom Johnston sold to Bournemouth for £12,000 in March 1973, was one of York City's best-ever strikers and another link to my old Club Manchester City where we played in the reserves together in 1964.

Looking back on that Walsall versus York City game in March 1973 it would have been ironic if I had scored just one of the chances and York had lost. Probably they would have gone down and the history of York City in the Second Division would not have happened.

My black humour thinks that maybe Tom Johnston bought me because I had inadvertently saved York from the drop. I like to think he saw the potential in me to score goals more often than I would miss them.

The Championship Year 1967/68

Team photo Man City 1967/68

Back Row: Tony Book, Stan Horne, George Heslop, Alan Ogley, Harry Dowd, Alan Oakes, Glyn Pardoe, Mike Doyle
Front Row: Mike Summerbee, David Connor, Colin Bell, Johnny Crossan, Chris Jones, Neil Young, Tony Coleman

Manchester City Tour of America

*Joe Mercer and
Chris Jones in Rochester,
New York*

*Niagara Falls –
Dave Connor and
Chris Jones*

City team in Atlanta, Georgia on steam boat

Bobby Kennedy and Chris Jones,
Chicago 1968

City in Atlanta 1968 Stan Horne, Neil Young, Chris Jones, Tony Book,
Glyn Pardoe George Heslop and Harry Dowd

City squad with baseball bats in Atlanta, Georgia

135

In between the Cities 1969–1973

Swindon Town League Cup squad and Promotion to Division 2 1968-69

Swindon Town – League Cup winner's celebration
Kensington Palace Hotel, London

Chris Jones in action at the county ground for Swindon

Swindon Town versus Derby County. Chris Jones and Roy McFarlane challenge for the ball

York City – The Football League 1973-74

Chris Jones and Ian Butler signing for York City in 1973.
Colin Meldrum the coach welcoming

City players in lighter mood at Pike Hills Golf Club.
Chris Jones 2nd from right

*Chris Jones celebrates
after scoring the
winning goal against
Huddersfield Town
April 1974*

*Taylor saves at the feet
of Chris Jones in vital 2-1
win in April 1974*

*Chris Jones 'shins' the
ball into title contenders
Bristol Rovers net for the
vital first goal
March 1974.
In memorable 2-1 win*

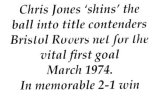

Chris Jones scores his 18th goal of the season against Brian Clough's Brighton at Bootham Crescent on 30th March 1974.

Tom Johnston tactics? Talk in 1974

Chris Jones with daughter Sheriden. Note the vinyl records

Chris Jones showing young daughter Sheriden how he scored
that historic goal

Chris Jones beats Goalkeeper Taylor of Huddersfield Town at Leeds Road but the ball hits the post.

Chris Jones heading into the Rochdale net January 5th 1974

In action again against Rochdale in a 2-1 win at Bootham Crescent

Chris Jones scoring the goal which secured York City's place in the 2nd Division (Championship) for the only time in its history. Ogden in the Oldham goal can only watch as the header enters the net

York City squad 1973-74

Graeme Crawford and York City's best ever 'Back four'.
Chris Topping, Barry Swallow, John Stone and Phil Burrows

The deadly strike force of Jimmy Seal and Chris Jones

York City's mid-field. John Woodward, Ian Holmes, Barry Lyons,
Cliff Calvert, and Brian Pollard. Ian Butler was injured with a broken leg but
played an important role in the promotion

Promotion celebrations on 27th April 1974. Chris Jones celebrates along with the ecstatic York Fans.

City, City, City roars the crowd gathered in front of the main stand at the end of the game

Celebrations in the dressing room as Director Gordon Winters passes out the champagne

Champagne moment for Chris Jones as he celebrates with team mates York City's most historic moment.

Yorks leading scorer Chris Jones with Steve Quinn York Rugby Leagues leading scorer for 1973-74 season

Graeme Crawford leading the after match celebrations

Chris Jones with Therese and daughter also share that champagne moment

A Tale of Two Cities – Bootham Crescent

John Stone, Chris Jones and Ian Butler leaving the Orient pitch after a 1-1 draw in the League Cup. Ian Butler would score the winner at Bootham Crescent which would set up the 'City' showdown

Jimmy Seal, Chris Jones and John Woodward dribble the balls down Moorcroft Road in York followed by excited fans before the Manchester City game at Bootham Crescent

Chris Jones left foot volley nearly wins the game for York City against his old club Manchester City at Bootham Crescent

Chris Jones with Mike Doyle and Tommy Booth in attendance.
Keith Macrae saves Chris's effort

Keith Macrae dives at the feet of Chris Jones at Bootham Crescent. Old team
mates Colin Bell and Glyn Pardoe in shot

Action at the Crescent
in 1973 as Chris Jones
and old adversary Mike
Doyle of Manchester City
challenge for the ball in the
Manchester Goal mouth.
Jimmy Seal (9)
and Rodney Marsh and
Colin Bell also in picture

A Tale of Two Cities – Maine Road

Keith Macrae of Manchester City saves at the feet of Chris Jones at Maine Road. Old team mate Glyn Pardoe has a watching brief

Chris Jones, Jimmy Seal and Mike Doyle of Manchester City can only watch as Brian Pollards shot ends up in the back of the net for Yorks' only goal

Aerial duel as Chris Jones, Mike Doyle and Keith Macrae challenge for the ball. Colin Bell and Tommy Booth watch anxiously as the goalkeeper punches it away

York City in the Second Division Championship

Chris Jones scores his first goal against Bobby Moore's Fulham at Craven Cottage in September 1974.

York City squad for the 1974-75 season.
The first and only time in Division 2

Chris Jones in York Cities Y fronts away strip in 1974-75

Chris Jones scoring with a diving header against Nottingham Forest away on November 23rd 1974. York City lost 2-1.

Chris Jones (far left) cracks a shot into the top left hand corner of the net against Milwall at Bootham Crescent. City won 2-1

Diving header attempt by Chris Jones against Aston Villa in the first game of the 2nd Division season at Bootham Crescent August 1974

Chris Jones challenges Alex Stepney of Manchester United 21st December 1974 at Bootham Crescent

Manchester United crowd being escorted along St Olaves Road to the ground in 1974.

Paul Hart of Blackpool (Johnny Harts son who was Chris Jones mentor at Manchester City) challenge for the ball?
At Bloomfield Road in September 1974.

Chris Jones third goal against Fulham at Craven Cottage as Peter Mellor goes to ground but disallowed.

*One of the many tussles
between Bobby Moore and
Chris Jones when they met in the
1974-75 and 1975-76 seasons*

*Chris Jones (far right)
scores the second goal
at Norwich City as
Jimmy Seal jumps
over the ball*

*Another goal for
Chris Jones against
Bobby Moores Fulham
but this time at Bootham
Crescent in March 1975.
Peter Mellor completely
dis-orientated*

Chris Jones scoring with a deflected shot past Old team mate at Swindon Town Peter Downsborough of Bradford City to win the second leg on aggregate 3-2

Chris Jones flashes a shot past Ray Clemence of Liverpool and England but just past the post in the League Cup at Bootham Crescent. Liverpool won the game with a penalty in the last minute 1-0

Chris Jones Left) with Bobby Moore of Fulham sees his shot on the way into the top corner of the net as Peter Mellor scrambles across goal at Bootham Crescent

Chris with Therese the day after he had dislocated his collar bone with a clash with Bristol City's Ray Cashley at Bristol City the night before.
York drew 0-0

The York City promotion side being introduced to thje Bootham Crescent faithful before the first game in the Second Division

Chris Jones (on left) applauds with his team mates Chris Topping as he receives the Clubman of the Year trophy

Chris Jones beats Peter Mellor in the Fulham goal for his second of the afternoon at Craven Cottage.

York City in 1975-76 season under Wilf McGuiness

Chris Jones volleys the ball into the net against Bradford City in the League Cup in 1975 for the winning goal

Chris Jones (10) and Jimmy Seal (9) in mid air ballet against West Bromwich Albion at Bootham Crescent

Roy Burton punches clear from Chris Jones, Oxford Utd 1975

Barry Siddall of Bolton Wanderers is beaten by Chris Jones for York City's only goal of the game losing 2-1 at Bootham Crescent

Chris Jones at Doncaster Rovers one of his later clubs

Chris (stripe) scoring for Rochdale in 1979 to preserve League status at the Club. Here he beats Kevin Rafferty in the Crewe goal watched by Ron Hilditch and Crewe player-manager Warwick Rimmer.

*Hat trick for Rochdale against Northampton Town at Spotland
30th October 1979*

Chris Jones with left to right Sheriden, Therese, Francesca and Calista.

The last days of Maine Road. Chris Jones celebrates with relations Daughter Francescas' Eighteenth birthday (3rd left) against Aston Villa.
Sadly Uncle Bill and daughter Sheriden could not make this final visit to one of my spiritual homes

Manchester Cities new home at the Etihad with Author Colin Schindler and Manchester United and Manchester City Youth players from 1963-64

Left to right: Dave Connor, Alf Wood, John Clay, Alan Ogley, Colin Schindler, Bobby Noble, Phil Burrows, Chris Jones, David Sadler

York City dropped like a stone after we played them and lost five of the next six games and drawing one. It took a goal from Jimmy Seal at Rotherham in a 2-1 win to keep York up by a decimal point. The Jones and Seal partnership had inadvertently helped to keep York City in Division Three but by the most strangest of happenings

I agreed to sign for York City and we went back to the ground for a medical and then to see George Teasdale, the Secretary, to complete the transfer.

I also managed to get a clause into the contract which gave me an added £10 a week pay rise at the end of the first year, a situation which caused a bit of furore amongst the other players when we were promoted.

I think it may have led indirectly to Phil Burrows not staying with the Club and going to Plymouth Argyle – in Phil's words, "as far away from Tom Johnston as possible." Still, for a Stockport lad that Phil was, I thought Plymouth was a bit extreme.

I phoned Ken Wheldon the Chairman of Walsall and said I had agreed to sign for York City and to go ahead with the deal, while also confirming our gentleman's agreement on the money and our removal arrangements to move to York.

We moved to York in late June of 1973 and immediately had a call from Tom Johnston to get down to Bootham Crescent for a photo-shoot with Jim Brownbill from the *York Evening Press* and to meet up with the Coach, Colin Meldrum.

Colin was a granite jawed Scotsman who didn't drink a lot but liked a lager to alleviate a back problem which kept acting up at certain times.

I had come across Colin when he was playing for Reading and remember a game against Swindon Town when he came up against one of my team mates Willie Penman. He jumped in with his left foot and took Willy at hip height, nearly carving him in two. The referee called him over for a booking, saying, "Colin I am going to report this as dangerous play or more exactly low flying and I think the latter is more appropriate."

Those were the days: Nowadays he would have got sent off and probably six months for aggravated assault.

Colin was an excellent coach and I found the link between the two Scotsmen very good. They were complete opposites in character, completely different, but the chemistry seemed to work.

Tom Johnston reminded me of George Poyser, the Manchester City Manager who signed me in 1964. Both were pipe-smoking dour individuals who kept to themselves and left it to the coaches to get the best out of the team.

Tom was in charge of York City for a long time, from October 1968 to January 1975. I believe he was the most successful Manager in York City's history.

Tom took over the Club while in the lower reaches of the Fourth Division and could not prevent them from having to apply for re-election to the Football League in 1969. Nowadays they would have automatically dropped into the Conference as York City were to later experience in 2004.

Tom was a very strict disciplinarian and was not particularly liked by a lot of the players. Having been under similar style managements I did not see this as a problem.

Tom had bought me and obviously had faith in what I could add to the Football Club. Prior to me signing, Tom had already moved the Club up to a respectable mid-table position in 1969-70 season and were to gain promotion to the Third Division the following year.

The next two seasons saw York City only survive relegation on goal average

When I signed at York the first thing Tom Johnston said was that I would be working with Colin Meldrum but as far as goal scorers at the Club was concerned I was the only one on the books.

Tom said that nobody at the Club had any confidence in scoring goals. I said "you can't put that on me." He said that York had forward players like Jimmy Seal who was brought in to score goals but had lost all confidence.

He stated but for an excellent defence and a zonal marking system we would have been relegated. I believed we stayed up by a decimal point.

Talking of zonal defences was completely foreign to me (maybe that was what I had run into in March at Fellows Park) and all I was interested in was holding the ball up, laying it off and getting back in the box and doing what I always liked – scoring goals. Tom said, "Nobody else will score, so Son you are going have to sort it out yourself."

Luckily that trip to the ground proved very positive for me as the new signing turned out to be Ian Butler, a left winger who had legendary status on the East Coast as the supplier of a stream of crosses for Ken Wagstaffe and Chris Chilton at Hull City.

Ian was first signed by Tom Johnston at Rotherham United straight from school but transferred on to Hull City for £40,000 in January 1965. He played 300 games for Hull and was a player I always looked with envy on when playing for Swindon Town against him.

Things were looking up and I always said if somebody can supply the ammunition I will fire the bullets. I got on very well with Ian and so did our wives Therese and Sylvia when the Butlers moved into a Club house across the road on the Woodthorpe Estate in York.

Colin told us that the signings were not over and they hoped to get somebody in on the right wing before the season started.

York did have a good young winger in Brian Pollard but I got the impression that experience was the key in staying away from the relegation places for the following season. They also fancied taking a young lad from Sheffield United called Ian Holmes.

YORK CITY FOOTBALL CLUB

Nec Cupias nec Metuas
Neither desire nor fear

So what was the history of this new City Club I was joining?

In 1908 the first York City Club was formed as an amateur concern and entered the Northern League and played out at Holgate Road. They entered the FA Amateur Cup and won two games against Withernsea and St Paul's before they went out of the cup against Scarborough in a local derby replay.

York had little success in the following two years and in the 1910-11 season in order to cut costs joined the Yorkshire Combination. Mr J F Wright became Secretary and realised that amateur football could not thrive in a rugby stronghold and signed a professional by the name of Corrighan, the first professional to play soccer for a club in the city of York. Mr Wright had bigger ideas and advocated the formation of a limited liability company to run a professional football club.

Several well known citizens expressed interest including the Lord Mayor of York, Alderman Norman Green who became York's first Chairman, Frank Marks who kept the Greyhound Hotel and Bert Rutter who ran the old Victoria Hall Cinema in Goodramgate.

York City evolved into a professional Club in 1912 and 592 five shilling shares were issued.

They played early games at Field View near Burton Stone Lane and the first game in front of 5,000 paying spectators was against Rotherham Town.

In May 1912 they were admitted to the Midland League and Peter Boyle, Sheffield United, Sunderland and Irish International, became the first Player-Manager at the Club.

After the initial enthusiasm for professional football the Club struggled in competition with fixture clashes with York RLFC. In August 1914 York City were invited to a meeting with the Nelson Club to discuss the formation of a Third Division of the Football League

They would have been one of the original founder members of the Football League Third Division. But the First World War intervened.

In 1917 the Club was put into liquidation through the bankruptcy court due to shortage of funds (where was Major William Sudell when we needed him)? So the end came after a brief five year history and it would be a further five years before the Club reformed as York City Football Club.

In May 1922 at a meeting in the Co-operative Hall a decision was made to form the York City Football and Athletic Club Limited and a letter was formulated to send to the Football League with the purpose of raising an Association Football Club. At the time the Club had neither players nor a football ground but still went ahead to try and join the Third Division North.

John Fisher and Secretary Harry Rusholme were sent to Football League Headquarters in London to plead York City's case. They were unsuccessful but they did manage one vote. Two months later they successfully applied for entry into the Midland League competition and then had a mad scramble to recruit players to turn out for the Club.

Also in the summer of 1922 the Club had financial problems and a shortage of funds to go into the Limited Company's share capital.

They came up with a scheme for the shares to be purchased on weekly instalments which led to many supporters becoming Shareholders.

These were the shares which ended up in the hands of Douglas Craig and his Board of Directors and nearly led to York City going out of existence in 2003.

The establishment of York City Football Club arose from a desire to provide sport for the working men at the British Railway yards and Rowntree's sweet factory amongst the many industries in the City and subsequently it became the working men of York who brought the Football Club into being.

On the 3rd June 1929, York City made their fourth attempt for League status and this time were successful and replaced Ashington in the Third Division North.

York City used a ground at Fulfordgate before moving to their spiritual home at Bootham Crescent in 1932.

The Club nearly went out of business in 2003 and suffered the ignominy of going out of the Football League in 2004 before returning in 2012.

So it was eight years in the wilderness of the Conference and a heart-rending time for all York City supporters until Gary Mills brought them back up through the play-offs in 2012 and a memorable win against Luton Town in the final at Wembley.

PRE-SEASON 1973

Sorting the goal scoring out was a problem I wrestled with for a week prior to pre-season training. Colin Meldrum alleviated some of my fears saying the Club was in good order and the team spirit was very good and also that we did have players who could score goals, but they just lacked confidence when chances arrived. Colin said we would work on a pattern of play linking me with Jimmy Seal up front.

Jimmy Seal was at Walsall at the time I was playing with Swindon Town and had gone on to play for Barnsley in 1971 scoring 12 goals in 43 league games.

He had moved to York City in July 1972 for a fee of £6,000 plus Kevin McMahon. However Jim was to have a really tough season with the Club and had even given way to John Stone in the centre forward position. Jim finished the season prior to my arrival with only four goals in 34 appearances. He did however score in the last game of the season at Rotherham to keep the Club in the Division.

We already had a left winger in place and I knew that Tom had gone back to Nottingham Forest and was trying to sign Barry Lyons on loan. The Club was not sure that they could get him.

Colin Meldrum and I both agreed that with two top class wingers and a link up with Jimmy Seal we could be in business. Colin said we were strong defensively but maybe needed somebody in mid-field.

So pre-season training started off with the usual grind of running and ball work. I found the players very welcoming and soon realised that this could be a very professional close knit squad.

Wrestling with the problem of goal scoring I devised a policy foreign to my nature. We used to run up to the Civil Service sports ground and then play matches with very small goals. I devised a plan and even now the lads still think I was a greedy player. All I did other than the running and training was hang around the goal I was attacking, smack the ball into the goal and celebrate in flamboyant fashion and shout, "What a great goal," and run around arrogantly with my arms in the air.

The lads used to say "get some work done you idle sod Jonesy" and I would reply, "No just give me the ball and let me score, you do the work and I will take the glory."

It was not really in my nature to be arrogant, but I was looking at Jimmy Seal thinking, "Come on, Jim, get nasty about things," and I could see he wanted a bit of this and the goal scoring and the elation that went with it.

He had done it in the past at Barnsley and my old Club Walsall, and just needed, like me, a structure and framework in which to work which would get us in goal-scoring positions.

During the pre-season Colin Meldrum worked with us on a pattern of play which could get the best out of the strike partnership.

In training Jimmy Seal blossomed; he had a great left foot and soon looked like a really quality striker and somebody I could link up with.

We did not have Barry Lyons at the time but still had Ian Butler on the left wing and Bryan Pollard on the right wing. So we walked through situations as a team, shadow playing the build up from the back and knowing where Sealy and I would move from any given part of the field.

In the build-up Jimmy and I would make at least three diagonal runs to finally end up at the business end in the opposition's box. For example if the ball was with John Stone (John had taken over from John Mackin who had gone to Corby Town) at right back, Sealy or myself would shorten to receive the ball in at feet. If it was played in then it was a lay-off and at least a 20 yard diagonal away. Meanwhile the other striker moved into the inside right channel to receive the ball and alternatives on that theme – it was flexible but always gave defenders and midfield the confidence that players were on the move. Defenders did not know whether to go with us on the run or pass us on to another defender and any hesitancy would leave us space and in 1973 and 1974 we had the players to deliver a "telling" pass.

Of course the main movement was clearing space for each other and the timing of the run into the box and leaving wide players with the confidence to play balls into space knowing one of us would be on the move trying to score, or at least put defenders off.

I already had played with Phil Burrows, a really good left back and to this day could not understand why he had not been retained by Manchester City after only one year as a professional. Phil had played left half in the Youth team at Manchester City with me during our run to the semi-finals and our meetings with Manchester United.

Phil joined York City in 1966 and by the time I arrived in 1973 was a hardened professional, now playing at left back, and with a promotion winning season behind him in 1970-1971. Phil did not miss a game in his last four seasons at York City and was the Club's first Clubman of the Year, a well deserved honour.

I always found that every good team had a few Scotsmen in it and we had Graeme Crawford in goal and John Woodward in midfield.

Graeme is arguably the best goalkeeper to have played for York City and is renowned for keeping 11 consecutive clean sheets in league matches which equalled the Football League record set up by Millwall in 1926. Again we might have an argument about my namesake Roger Jones or Tommy Forgan as the best goalkeeper to have been between the sticks at York City.

I will stick my neck out and say that Graeme Crawford was the best line goalkeeper I have played with and that includes my Manchester City team mates Alan Ogley and Bert Trautmann (although I only played with Bert at the end of his fabulous career).

Obviously with a zonal marking system you do not want your goalkeeper going AWOL on the penalty spot so Graeme stayed on his line and reacted to each situation as it arose. A typical Scotsman:

172

didn't like to give anything away and that particularly went for goals in his net.

John Stone played right back with what was a quality and seasoned centre back pairing in Chris Topping and Barry Swallow. However I already knew what abilities this defence had after my game against them for Walsall in March 1973.

John had made a couple of Second Division appearances for Middlesbrough before signing for York City in July 1972. He established himself in the right back position but had to fight John Mackin for the position and ended up playing a few games at centre forward in 1972 and scoring five goals.

There was no argument about York City's best centre back pairing of all time – Barry Swallow and Chris Topping. Topps was York City's first apprentice professional. He made his League debut as a 17 year old in December 1968 and soon established himself in the side. Chris was a very consistent performer and although both strong in the tackle and good in the air always seemed to come out of games unscathed.

He had the most vicious slide/scissor tackle I have witnessed (ask Bruce Bannister of Bristol Rovers who managed to get himself sent off after a Topps tackle) and was the Back Four's quiet assassin while always being so polite to the referee and to opponents. Topps was also my roommate and responsible for me having tea and toast in bed every Saturday morning prior to a game. A good all-round professional was Topps, although I would have liked a spot of marmalade on the toast.

He had York City's captain and centre half Barry Swallow as his mentor and they were a formidable partnership long before I appeared at York City. Barry, a very experienced performer was a great motivator with similar characteristics to Malcolm Allison at Manchester City. He could lead by example but also get a little bit more out of players in the team by his confidence and slightly aggressive and arrogant attitude.

Barry had started at Doncaster Rovers then went on to play for Crewe Alexandra, Barnsley and Bradford City before he arrived at York City in February of 1969 for a fee of £3,000. Barry went on to lead the York City side to promotion in 1970-71 and was to be an ever present in the 1973-74 season.

John Woodward would be the anchor man in midfield during 1973-74. John was a Glaswegian and Scottish Youth International and signed for Arsenal in January 1966. He only managed three appearances for Arsenal and was signed by York City in July 1971. John took a while to settle and it wasn't until the 1972-73 season that he established himself in the team. In the 1973-74 season he made 38 appearances for the Club and was probably the unsung hero in our team.

Dennis Wann who played on the left wing at the time was out with a broken leg sustained at Chesterfield. He had been bought for a £7,000 fee in 1972 from Blackpool and only managed a few games at the back end of the 1973/74 season. He had a wicked sense of humour of which I was to be a victim in Iceland and on a tour of Majorca.

Brian Pollard was a local lad who signed for York City as a professional in March 1972. He was a very direct winger and started the 1973-7 season in the side but had to compete as the season wore on with our two experienced wing-men Barry Lyons and Ian Butler. However Brian was an important member of the squad and made 21 appearances and 6 substitute appearances for us.

Cliff Calvert and Brian Pollard were to play a significant part in our 1973-1974 campaign. Cliff, like Brian, was capped at Youth International level for England and signed as a full time professional in July 1972. Cliff could either play midfield or full back and played a significant role in the squad with 32 appearances that year.

John Peachey was a strong centre forward who was the main cover for Jimmy Seal and me and made four very important League contributions and scored a winning goal against Wrexham in my absence, and a goal each against Shrewsbury and Southport in that season.

Ron Hillyard was our understudy goalkeeper. Ron joined York City as a junior and made his debut in 1969. He made 34 appearances in the promotion winning season of 1970-71 but lost confidence just at the time of Graeme Crawford's loan signing from Sheffield United in November 1971.

Graeme signed for the Club in December of 1971 and for the next five and a half seasons was nearly an ever present in the first team and wasn't to miss a game along with Chris Topping in our two years in the Second Division.

However the jig-saw was not complete as we prepared for the new season with a trip to Scotland to play Dunfermline and Morton before returning for a game against Sheffield United.

Morton, I should have realised, was maybe the talisman to a good season as I scored in pre-season at Swindon in 1969 and again repeated the feat with two goals against them in 1973.

Ian Holmes joined at the start of the regular season and became an absolute God-send for us. We called him Wobbles and he had an abundance of skill but typically was a cocky young player with a fair bit to learn. He had come like Graeme Crawford from Sheffield United where he made six appearances before arriving at Bootham Crescent.

Ian was our penalty expert along with Barry Lyons, Ian Butler and John Woodward. Sealy and me wanted to take penalties to boost our goal tallies but were well down the pecking order in this team. We used to nip forward and put the ball on the penalty spot hoping for a chance but were always dragged away by the team. They had seen us on the training ground practising penalties and were plainly not too impressed with our efforts. We always lived in hope, but were never called up to shoot from the spot. I actually scored my only penalty for Manchester City Reserves in a match at Elland Road against Leeds United in 1965. That experience did not seem to impress my team mates and I even think they had me back of Graeme Crawford in the pecking order which was a real insult (although Graeme thought that was about right).

My nearest chance was when Bobby Moore brought me down in the box at the Crescent and Barry Lyons was off the pitch, Ian Butler injured and Wobbles looking knackered on the halfway line. When I nipped to put the ball on the penalty spot I have never seen a player recover so quickly and sprint 50 yards into the Fulham penalty area.

I looked up and saw Barry Swallow's look of relief when I relinquished possession to Wobbles. Needless to say Ian Holmes converted the penalty we won 1-0 and my only opportunity for penalty fame to my disgust went down the drain. The rest of the team looked quite relieved.

However, Wobbles gave the team an added impetus with strong runs at defenders and also gave us the option of a Third Man making runs into the heart of opposition defences.

The making of Ian Holmes was when Barry Lyons joined us from Nottingham Forest in September 1973.

Barry's first appearance was against Port Vale in a 3-1 win when he was on loan to us, but soon he signed for the season. At that point in time we had a solid squad and were confident that the season might be a reasonable one.

THE SEASON BEGINS 1973

Our first game of the season was away to Charlton Athletic at The Valley. I remember it with affection as it was a sweltering day in London, 85 degrees, tough for footballers but memorable for a 4-2 win and my first goal for York City. John Woodward who had played for Arsenal enjoyed his return to London and scored two goals. However the most important one for me was Jimmy Seal's goal as it gave me the feeling that we had a formidable partnership in progress and that Tom Johnston's words that the onus would have to be on me to score the goals in the York City team may not be necessarily so.

We came back to Bootham Crescent cock-a -hoop but were soon brought down to earth drawing against Halifax Town 1-1.

However, it was a memorable match for me as I scored my first goal for York City at Bootham Crescent. A cross from the left by Ian Butler and a right foot volley from 12 yards gave us a share of the points. Blackburn Rovers away gave us a reality check with a 4-0 thrashing and some hard words were said amongst us after that affair.

However that was to become one of the strengths of our squad: we could give and take criticism without malice.

Tom Johnston usually stayed out of these situations and let the players and Colin Meldrum thrash it out amongst themselves. Obviously it had come as a shock, especially for a defence that prided itself in being Scrooge-like in giving goals away. However we were in it as a team with the front men being the first line of defence and we also had duties during set plays in our zone-marking defensive roles.

Well, in these players' meetings, usually led by the captain Barry Swallow, something must have been put right as we went on a long run of clean sheets during October and November.

It is still a club record to this day that we went eleven games in a season without conceding a goal. Millwall in 1926 held the record which we equalled.

Aldershot on September 29th 1973 was the last goal anybody scored against us for the next eleven games and it was at Aldershot on December 22nd when we finally conceded a couple of goals in a 2-2 draw. Jimmy Seal and me were glad when we finally let one in as we felt the record was becoming an albatross around our necks.

The press had started to go on about beating the Millwall 1926 record and we were going into our shell as a team and lost a lot of our attacking flair as we started to defend ever deeper in the final couple of games.

However the week before this we did stick four goals past Southport at Bootham Crescent and Sealy and me got on the sheet. So we were feeling pleased and confident about our trip down to Aldershot.

However the next home match after the Blackburn debacle was a "grudge" match for me as Walsall were due at York and I had an old score to settle with Stan Bennett after our altercations months earlier at Walsall.

Things never seem to work out as you want and I had a telephone call at the ground from the Chairman of Walsall, Mr Wheldon, saying that he had a "present" for me and would like to see me before the kick-off. Avarice took over – Stan Bennett took a back seat as did my attempt to concentrate on a clean sheet after our drubbing at Blackburn Rovers.

Fifteen minutes before kick-off I was asked to pop out of the dressing room as the Walsall Chairman wished to speak to me.

I put on a track suit top and nipped out of the door and met the Chairman. He thanked me for moving, and as per our gentleman's agreement handed me an envelope, which he assured me had £1,500 in it. We shook hands, wished each other luck and I stuffed the envelope under my track suit and tried nonchalantly to walk back into the dressing room under what I thought was the inquisitive gaze of the players.

I uncomfortably waited while the final team talk was done by Colin Meldrum followed by a few words of encouragement from Tom, and then surreptitiously slipped the envelope out of my track suit and into my boot locker, still not knowing whether the correct amount of money was there.

I was last out of the dressing room and made sure that the apprentices locked the door and I was first back in at half-time and full-time just to assure myself that the envelope was still in the locker.

It was, but to my chagrin I forgot my vendetta with Stan Bennett and tried my best to concentrate on the game. We came out of the game with a 1-1 draw, with Ian Butler scoring our goal – but no clean sheet. But the money was in the envelope.

Anyway I thought I might get a few kicks in against Bennett at Fellows Park as we were due to play them again in October. Well, fate conspired against me as we won three and drew two of our next games with me scoring at Chesterfield but then getting knee ligament damage against Aldershot and missing five games, including Walsall.

So Stan Bennett and myself never did lock horns again as we moved up a Division in 1974.

Aldershot, which we won 3-1, was the last time anybody scored in the league against us until December 20th when we drew 2-2 at Aldershot. In those days of two points for a win and one for a draw, clean sheets and drawn games kept you in the top part of the leagues if you could win at home.

John Peachey deputised for me and Tom Johnston was losing patience with my rehabilitation and thought I was pandering to the injury a bit. I thought I was on the mend from medial ligament damage – but not quickly enough for Tom.

He had me in the office and said, "We will put a strapping on your leg and give you a cortisone injection before the game."

I said, "I think it will be fine for the Brighton game away."

Tom said, "You will play against Tranmere Rovers as we are missing your goals and link up play with Jimmy Seal and if you don't we may have to put you under the knife and see what is wrong."

Needless to say the thought of any surgery and anybody having a cut at my knee motivated me, and I dutifully turned out and with Tom's man-management skills we managed to win 2-0.

I had been out of the side for five games and the team had five clean sheets, but had only scored one goal in my absence.

The following week we went to Brighton and it was the legendary Brian Clough's first game in charge. We drew 0-0 in front of 16,000 fans. From our point of view it was trying to put one over on a legend of the game, and our clean sheets continued with the draw.

After the Brighton game we came back to play Southend United and won 1-0. I scored one of my favourite forms of goal, a diving header, this time from a fizzed-in cross from Barry Lyons from the right wing which gave us the two points. It was a welcome relief after coming back from ligament damage and Tom Johnston's threat of the knife. Even now I keep giving my right knee a rub at the thought of it – no keyhole surgery then.

At Shrewsbury the following week we had a massive set-back with Ian Butler breaking his leg, a bitter blow to a side which relied on good wing play, and Ian would be out until the beginning of April. However this gave Brian Pollard, one of our younger players, a chance to come into the breach for some games and also Denis Wann to make a return from his broken leg in February.

Ken Mulhearn, the Shrewsbury goalkeeper, was at Manchester City with me and it was quite an eventful reunion. I scored our first goal with John Peachey scoring the second in a 2-0 win. I was running through on Ken's goal trying to score a second, when he came out and flew in with his studs showing , slashing me across the right wrist which left a six inch scar to this day. The ball went past the post. When I go to the Etihad for the Manchester City former players' dinner, I still have a dig at Ken about fearless goalkeepers.

I scored in a 4-0 home win against Southport the following week with Jimmy Seal, Brian Pollard and John Peachey also on the score sheet.

Jimmy Meadows was the Manager of Southport and he along with John Hart had been coaches at Manchester City in my amateur days at Chassen Road in Urmston. I have a diary entry from Tuesday 17th September 1963 which just said *Training with Jimmy (Meadows) – rugged!* Jimmy was another coach who used to make it tough for us in the Maine Road gymnasium with numerous two-a-side skittle ball matches, Hart and Meadows versus Jones and Connor, epics! So we knew what to expect from a Jimmy Meadows side: no quarter asked or given.

In the Southport ranks that day were Clive Clark, the West Brom Albion and Preston winger who had just recovered from a broken leg, my old colleague from Manchester City days Tony Coleman (no hugs and kisses on this occasion) and an ex-York City player Andy Provan who had scored 21 goals the season before for Southport.

While we were striving to stretch our remarkable defensive record of not conceding a goal to eleven games, Southport were trying to stop a run of six successive away defeats

The following week the long run of clean sheets in the League came to an end at Aldershot where we came back to draw 2-2.

A coincidence was that Jack Howarth had scored for Aldershot at Bootham Crescent when we beat them 3-1. That was on the 29th September 1973 and it was Jack Howarth who scored at Aldershot on the 22nd December 1973 to end our amazing run.

After that we won three games, drew three games and lost 1-0 to Charlton as we went through into 1974 in the heady heights of the top positions with 34 points. The York City Club record of 21 games undefeated in a season still stands to this day although the present side under Nigel Worthington has gone on a long run in Division Two in 2014 with 17 unbeaten performances to the end of the 2013/14 season.

However, we came down to earth with a bump, losing that 21 game record with a home defeat to Charlton Athletic at home 1-0.

This was the first year when the first three teams in the League would gain promotion.

Looking back at the first part of that season I realised that a lot of things had to come together to make it what was to be one of the best teams in York City's history.

Of course there was the enigma of Tom Johnston. I had not realised when I came to the Club that in his first year York City had to apply for re-election to the Football League.

Now it is automatic relegation to the Conference (as York fans are well aware, after our eight years in the wilderness and near extinction from the Football League pyramid).

Tom improved the squad and they got promotion to the Third Division in 1970-1971 season but only stayed up on goal average in the next two seasons. Being a strict Scottish disciplinarian, he was not really liked by most of the players. His Coach at the time was Billy Horner who was a good coach and liked by the players.

Phil Burrows told me that they detested Tom but liked Billy Horner and that a major row had developed over various issues in the team dressing room. After a team meeting the players led by Barry Swallow had put a vote of no confidence in Tom Johnston as Manager. Somehow the matter was eventually resolved, Billy Horner leaving and Colin Meldrum arriving from Reading as the new Coach.

It is only now as I look back at these times that there was always an undercurrent of distaste from the players who had stayed on with regards to Tom Johnston. Although the dressing room was split it did not affect the training and the playing. From somewhere it drew the squad into a tightly knit unit and one of the quotes was "in spite of him" (Tom) "we will succeed."

Colin Meldrum was really the unsung hero of the piece as he had to take the place of the well liked Billy Horner and guide the team through to the end of the season. He then had to find some common ground between the retained players of 1973, Tom Johnston, and the newly signed players like me, Ian Butler, Ian Holmes and Barry Lyons.

Well, the chemistry, volatile though it was, seemed to work, and the uneasy peace did not seem to affect what was happening on the pitch.

THE CLASH OF THE TWO CITIES

Et collisione duorum

The FA Cup came and went in November and December 1973. On 24th November we drew 0-0 with Mansfield at Bootham Crescent in front of over 4,000 fans.

A fortnight later we went to Mansfield for the replay and were two goals up after seven minutes but lost 5-3.

Barry Swallow had put a long ball down the middle of the field and Sealy headed it on and I scored with a low cross shot into the net after three minutes. We were two up after seven minutes when Brian Pollard's free kick was deflected, the goalkeeper couldn't hold it and Barry Swallow put it into the empty net.

But a confident Mansfield team then stuffed five goals past us before I finally got my second goal of the night when Brian Pollard crossed fiercely into the box and I deflected it into the net. Maybe we had become complacent having just equalled Millwall's record of so many league games without conceding a goal.

Our usual inquest on the game put it down to too many silly individual errors and we all hoped we could learn from what had happened. I felt that it was the strength of our squad that we could bounce back as individuals and also as a team.

We were very positive as a group, and Colin Meldrum reminded us of how consistent we had been in the League. He reminded us that we had only lost three out of the last 33 games and that was promotion-winning form.

The League Cup was a different kettle of fish. We had beaten Huddersfield Town 1-0 with an own goal on August 29th and had beaten Aston Villa 1-0 with a John Peachey goal on 9th October.

I missed that game with medial ligament damage but was back in time to play against Orient away on the 31st October.

We came out of London with a 1-1 draw with Barry Swallow getting the goal. The replay was the following week on 6th November in front of over 11,000 fans and it went into extra time. Ian Holmes scored and then Ian Butler got the winner.

I was off the field with a slight injury when Ian sent the fans delirious with his goal. But no one was more delirious than me and Phil Burrows as we realised that it would be the dream match-up against Manchester City in the next round at Bootham Crescent.

Sadly for Ian Butler he would break his leg two weeks later at Shrewsbury and miss the Manchester City game, due to be played on the 21st November 1973.

While we were waiting for the collision of the two Cities in the League Cup the Country was heading for what was to be known as the 'Big Blackout'. This was when the threat of the lights going out all over Britain was a distinct possibility.

The National Grid had warned that demand for electricity could reach 95 per cent of available supplies if we were hit by a prolonged cold spell similar to 1972 or worse the Big Freeze of 1962-63 which shut football down for three months.

The crisis came before we beat Orient. The Arab States launched a surprise attack on Israel in October and the subsequent war quadrupled oil prices. Arab countries reduced the supplies to the West and with the price of coal rising and stocks dwindling in Britain the miners rejected a pay increase and voted for a National strike. Then on the 12th November miners and electricity workers began an overtime ban. The Chancellor, Anthony Barber, thought the Country could survive a coal strike for a while and also high oil prices for a while but not the two together. Andrew Marr in his book *The History of Modern Britain* called it the greatest economic crisis since the 1939-1945 war.

York were playing Hereford at home and we were engaged in a 0-0 draw which was the eighth consecutive game in the League without a goal being scored against us. The following day Edward Heath declared a state of emergency. The use of electricity for floodlighting, advertising and the heating of shops, offices and restaurants were banned.

Football was hit, with mid-week games having to be called off or played in the afternoon with smaller crowds. A backlog of fixtures developed.

On the 17th November we travelled to Shrewsbury Town and won 2-0, John Peachey and I scoring the goals. It was another clean sheet but this was the game in which Ian Butler broke his leg and was then out for most of the season.

We didn't have a League game until the 8th December when, as mentioned earlier, we beat Southport 4-0 at home. A fortnight later our long run of clean sheets came to an end at Aldershot.

On the 20th November the Government ordered all oil companies to cut deliveries to private and industrial consumers by ten per cent. By staying neutral in the dispute between Israel and the Arab countries we luckily avoided the oil embargo put on the USA and Holland. However the situation was drastic enough, and the Post Office started to issue petrol coupons to motorists. The police were on the look-out for petrol hoarders, 180 gallons of fuel being found in a company director's garage. His quote to the police was: "I don't think you will believe It's for the lawn mower then?" He got a £60 fine.

The next day we played Manchester City at Bootham Crescent with a 2pm kick off to get the game in before darkness. Looking back, I wonder if the Manchester City players had to hand over their petrol coupons to get the coach over the Pennines for the match and back to Manchester afterwards?

The Manchester City team had all my old friends in the line-up – Colin Bell, Francis Lee, Tommy Booth and Glyn Pardoe. Glyn had made a comeback after that horrific over-the-top tackle by George Best in the Manchester derby at Old Trafford in 1971.

I was up against Tommy Booth and the late Mike Doyle. Mike had played in the same Youth team at Manchester City with Phil Burrows and me. Doyley was not one of the players who I particularly liked and I still remember him for stoking up the game against Manchester United Youths which led to it being less of a spectacle and more of a kicking match at Old Trafford in front of 35,000 fans.

The game was played on a cold and gloomy afternoon in front of nearly 16,000 spectators. The stories given of how people got off work and school for the match that afternoon are numberless. I had my hip replaced in 2006 and my anaesthetist said he was at St Peter's school and bunked it with quite a few friends to watch the game. He said the licking was worth it and I was in good hands for the operation.

The headline from the game at Bootham Crescent was that Tommy Booth's nose saved Manchester City from being victims of a giant-killing. Jimmy Seal had crossed the ball into the box and I caught it on the volley with my left foot and thought the goalkeeper, Keith Macrae, had no chance of saving it. But it blasted into the face of Tommy Booth and flew off towards the goal line. The memorable quote from Tommy to the press was, "It caught me on de dose." Mike Doyle, gracious as always, said it would have missed anyway.

It was disappointing that the shot did not hit the back of the net to knock my old Club out of the competition. As a team we didn't do ourselves justice that afternoon, but I was surprised they played so defensively against us. They were definitely not the team that played in such a cavalier fashion under Malcolm Allison and Joe Mercer when I was there.

Tony Book, who was in charge for the game, was pleased with the result and to get us back to Maine Road. My old mates Francis Lee and Mike Summerbee both had chances to beat us but maybe the old sparkle was leaving them and their best years were behind them. Colin Bell probably had the best chance, lobbing just over Graeme Crawford's crossbar, although Rodney Marsh could have settled it with more power in a last minute shot.

The accolade to York City was the quote from Tony Book, saying that he was pleased with the result and admitted the gap between the First Division and the Third Division was not near as wide as it used to be. Tony was probably remembering our trip to the States in 1968 when Malcolm compared the Atlanta Chiefs to a Fourth Division outfit and we lost twice to them. Diplomatically no mistake was being made on that afternoon.

THE REPLAY AT MAINE ROAD

Secundo collisione urbes

A fortnight later on the Wednesday 5th December we went back to my first love, Maine Road, for a nostalgic replay. All the events of that trip to Maine Road are as vivid today as they were on that cold dark murky evening.

As we approached the ground looking very gloomy with the lack of street lighting and only the roar of the generators and the lights from the floodlights to lift the stillness of Moss Side, my mind went back to that moment when I first came to sign for Manchester City in 1962.

The old ground still had a fascination for me and memories flooded back and I was filled with emotion as the coach drove up Platt Lane, threading its way through the gathering crowd and up to the players' entrance. How many times I had approached this door and gone through I could not count, but I had the feeling that this would be the last time I entered Maine Road as a player and it sent shivers down my spine.

Through the players' entrance we went but then not a right turn into the home dressing room, but to the left where many years ago the apprentices and reserves used to change for training. Memories swept back but now I was a professional Footballer and my aim was to put my old Club out of the League Cup if I could.

A crowd of 18,000 was there. What a fantastic reception we got as we ran out under the floodlights and wonderful moments of Youth Cup glories and goals flooded back to remind me what a great Club I had played for, giving me many of my best footballing memories.

We fancied our chances of at least taking them to extra-time, and in the first half we gave them a game although we gifted them the first goal. Graeme Crawford was in good form early on, turning Mike Summerbee's long cross over the bar and Colin Bell heading over from a Rodney Marsh cross. We thought we had weathered the early City storm when Leman crossed into the box and both Topps and Stoney left it for one another and John Peachey (what was he doing back there) tried to poke it back to Graeme Crawford but only succeeded in passing it to Rodney Marsh who gleefully rounded Graeme and put it into the empty net.

But we were level four minutes later when Brian Pollard hit a great shot on the half-volley from a John Woodward corner which flew past a crowd of players including me into the back of Keith Macrae's net. This was the best half we had played in a while, and although Phil Burrows had to clear off the line from a Tony Towers header we reached half-time on top with Barry Lyons putting in a great cross which John Woodward drove over the bar.

We said what we always said in the dressing room: the next ten minutes would be important and we had to keep them out at all costs.

Easier said than done: after only two minutes we were 2-1 down and a tough night looked like getting tougher against this star-studded side. John Stone had put the ball into touch just opposite our area and a quick throw left us one short defensively. Tony Towers flicked the ball to Francis Lee who beat Graeme from ten yards out only to find Phil Burrows on the line saving with his hand. Penalty given, though in those days it was not an automatic sending off.

Franny Lee, who was unerring with all his penalties, duly despatched the ball into the right hand corner of Graeme's net and we feared we were in for a mauling.

Manchester played some good football after that, but we tried to match them and we broke on a couple of occasions, Brian Pollard shooting wide and John Peachey doing the same when a pass to me would have given me an easy chance to score at my old Club. To say that I stared daggers at Peachey was an understatement and I gave him plenty of verbals for being greedy.

That was that on the night for us and after an hour's play Rodney Marsh got his second, playing a one-two with Francis Lee and scoring off a post.

Graeme made a good save from Towers and Phil again chested a ball off the line before Rodney Marsh completed his hat-trick. The cuttings say that Barry Lyons fouled Francis Lee 25 yards out (impossible, as Barry never tackled – we called him Jensen after the car – Jensen Interceptor). Marsh hit the shot and it took a deflection off Topps and cruelly went through Graeme's legs into the net. We were outclassed in the second half by a side sprinkled with Internationals looking for a trip to Wembley.

I managed to have a short nostalgic chat with my mentor Jonny Hart at the players' entrance where so many years ago I had knocked on the door when I first came to sign as an amateur for Manchester City and was told by Dave Ewing to come back on Thursday as training was off that evening.

John, who had not been well and had to give up the Manager's job at City, was recuperating and in good spirits when I was called to travel back over the Pennines. Tom Johnston was trying to hurry me onto the bus but I was not going to be rushed and said, "Leave me here, then, but I am finishing my conversation with Harty."

Finally we said our goodbyes and feeling melancholy I left Maine Road for the last time as a player. As the coach left Maine Road and made its way into the fog and mist of the Manchester night I thought, even though we had lost 4-1, Phil and I had come back to Manchester City and proved our credibility as professional players.

The League Cup journey was over for us but we still had a lot to play for as 1973 came to a close and the Blackout continued. Manchester City would go on to reach the final of the League Cup in March 1974 where they came up against Wolverhampton Wanderers and lost 2-1. Colin Bell had equalised a Hibbitt goal before John Richards got the winner five minutes from time.

Back home to York and power cuts became part of our everyday lives. Power cut timetables were published in the Evening Press and Therese, Sheriden and I were well prepared for the inconvenience. We had got in the Calor gas and paraffin heaters and even with Heath's prediction of a hard winter ahead everyone decided we were going to have a good time. The football was still going ahead but without the mid-week games, and early kick-offs became the norm.

Like most people in Britain we "dug in" and made the best of the situation. The York City wives got together and organised a séance as a form of entertainment. Strange, but I don't remember them mentioning what was in the future for the football team in 1974.

The Christmas number one for 1973 was Merry Christmas everyone by Slade. Its lyrics captured the mood of all of us: So here it is, Merry Christmas, everybody's having fun touched the irony of the situation we were all in. Comedians made the most of it and Bruce Forsyth on his show said: "It could come to this," struck a match and said, "Match of the day."

THE RUN IN 1974

Elit ad dimicandum in foedus.
A fight to the finish in the League

So we went into the second half of the season out of both the League Cup and the FA Cup. In the League we were jolted by Charlton Athletic beating us 1-0 on our own ground. A reality check needed to be taken by the team.

We had another "thrash it out", session behind closed doors with Colin Meldrum. Tom Johnston had seen it all before and stayed out of it: he realised that we had a lot of experienced but volatile players in the dressing room and that any intervention by him would be incendiary.

In the next game we bounced back and got a 3-1 win at Rochdale on 4th February and I got a couple of goals and Jimmy Seal the other one. Always a favourite ground for me was Spotland, having scored for Manchester City in my early days in the Lancashire League and I was to finish off my career with Rochdale, getting a hat-trick against Northampton Town in my final season.

So, no better place for the team to get back on the winning track. Travelling back over the M62 in the evening was joyous and the team were in high spirits. We were still not contemplating promotion as there were so many good teams in the Division, with both Oldham and Bristol Rovers forcing the pace with Wrexham and Chesterfield close behind.

The following day we awoke to the terrible news that a bomb had gone off in a coach on the M62 near Hartshead Services and killed twelve people – nine soldiers and three civilians. It turned out that the IRA had planted the bomb in the coach that was carrying off-duty

British Armed Service personnel and their family members. *There but for the grace of God go I* goes the saying and I contemplated the horror that had been perpetrated just six hours after we had gone across that same motorway.

The coach had left Manchester and was heading for Catterick Garrison when the bomb exploded. It still brings shivers to my spine today as I contemplate that near miss and the events of our coach travelling to West Bromwich Albion later that same year on 5th October 1974.

In our next match we drew with Watford at home 2-2 then lost to Wrexham 1-0 away, a game which saw Ron Hillyard in goal for Graeme Crawford. The end of February and early March became a crucial time for us but we bounced back and won the next three games against Cambridge Athletic 2-0, Grimsby Town 2-1 and Bournemouth 3-1. In the latter game I thought I had scored but it was given to Chris Topping, but was reclaimed by me at the end of the season.

We drew at Tranmere Rovers 0-0 and then lost a keenly contested match at Boundary Park in front of 15,806 fans against our big local rivals from across the Pennines, Oldham Athletic, 2-1. Phil Burrows scored the consolation goal in the game getting his second nose bleed of the campaign after coming over the half-way line.

It was not enough and we had the league leaders Bristol Rovers visiting the Crescent the following week. It was to become the crucial moment in the season, when the top three teams could perhaps break away from the pack.

We were in second place behind Rovers. The fans turned out in force and in front of a crowd of over 11,000 we managed to win 2-1. It was a game of high drama with me scoring the first goal in the 52nd minute. Ian Holmes had wobbled past three defender's down the left wing and crossed the ball into the box and I struck it into the roof of the net. It was nearly a miss as I 'shinned it' onto the underside of the bar and into the net. Sometimes I think of that moment and still say to myself: "what if I'd missed it?"

Ian Holmes ran through the defence after that and should have put the game to bed but he hit the crossbar. In the 81st minute Bruce Bannister got himself sent off for retaliation on Chris Topping (he didn't like one of Topps's tackles). Down to ten men, they shocked us by equalising in the 85th minute and all the good work of the season could have come undone. However it was to be a sensational finish: in the fifth minute of injury time John Woodward was barged to the ground in the box as a right wing corner came in.

That caused an uproar in the Bristol Rovers ranks as a penalty was given and Stephens (who had scored the equaliser) protested too much and referee Whalley from Southport sent him off. When the uproar died down Ian Holmes coolly slotted home the penalty. Well, it was a remarkable match, won with the last kick of the game, taking us to within three points of Rovers at the top of the table with a game in hand. For the first time, we saw the possibilities of going from near relegation in 1973 to promotion in 1974.

This was the time when the experience of the team came to the fore. We all got together and said: "It has to be one game at a time – do not look further ahead."

We then went on our travels to play Southend on a Sunday and got a 3-3 draw with me getting two goals and Jimmy Seal getting the other.

We stayed down on the South Coast for a mid-week game against Bournemouth and came away with a 3-1 win with Jimmy Seal, Ian Holmes and me again on the score sheet. This was turning out to be a rich goal scoring vein for the team and for me in particular, and came at just the right time for our promotion push.

Back to Bootham Crescent to play our third South coast team in Brian Clough's Brighton at the end of March. I scored two goals this time and we won 3-0. Phil Burrows, with his third nose bleed of the campaign, scored the other.

For the second goal I was put through with nearly half the field to run and plenty of time to think how I was going to beat the keeper as I closed in on him. Goal-scoring instincts took over and as the keeper advanced I slotted it right-footed past him and into the net at the Shipton Street end of the ground.

I indulged in a bit of an elaborate celebration running back to the halfway line and I arrogantly stopped in front of Mr Clough. I don't think he was too pleased, but as a goal scorer himself for

Sunderland he could probably accept my elation if not the arrogance of the moment. Our gates were averaging between 7,000 and 10,000 supporters and suddenly people in York were becoming aware that something special was happening down at the Football Club.

We were still talking caution amongst the team but we were a confident outfit and Graeme Crawford with our back four of John Stone, Chris Topping, Barry Swallow and Phil Burrows were all having consistently good performances which gave the rest of the lads great confidence. In front of them we had consistently good performances from John Woodward anchoring in front of the back four and then Holmes, Pollard, Lyons and Butler providing the ammunition for Jimmy Seal and me to fire the bullets. For forwards, it's nice to know that on a lot of occasions you might only need one goal to take both points.

We only drew 1-1 against Plymouth with Jimmy Seal getting the goal and followed it up with another draw at Hereford 0-0 and our cause for a bit of concern was there for all to see.

So there was another team meeting with Colin and another rallying call to stick together as it was in our hands to get promotion.

Every time we had these meetings it seemed to inspire us and I again managed to come up with the goods against our local rivals Huddersfield Town 2-1. Ian Holmes scored the first from the penalty spot (another attempt by me to get hold of the ball and take a penalty but to no avail). I scored a late and welcome winner for the team to take both points in front of nearly 10,000 worried but finally ecstatic fans at Bootham Crescent.

The finishing line was getting closer and like all teams in York City's history we gave the fans late drama and anguish. We lost a home game to Shrewsbury Town 1-0. Mortification! Was the chalice of Division Two football going to be poisoned at the death?

We had to go to Huddersfield Town in the next game (the second of two Bank Holiday fixtures against them) and fought for everything. The lads kept a clean sheet and my strike partner Jimmy Seal produced the only goal of the game. We were back in the hunt, not only for promotion but maybe for the Championship too.

We travelled to lowly Southport on the 19th April, wary of a banana skin from a team with very little left to play for. Barry Lyons scored and we got out with an honourable draw.

It was three games to go to push York City into the fantasy world of the Second Division and peaks climbed nobody had ever thought possible.

The 27th April 1974 was to be a historic day in my footballing career. We were in third position in the League with Bristol Rovers top and Oldham in second place. The way the results had worked out, it was possible that we could be promoted if we avoided a home defeat by Oldham. We were now a really confident set of players and our aim was to beat them and try and win the League.

The big day dawned bright and sunny and we came out to a crowd of 15,583. What a reception the teams received as they came out onto the Bootham Crescent pitch.

I still remember the game to this day (highlights can be seen in archive footage on *You Tube*). The first half had a dramatic start when Wood of Oldham dislocated his collar bone and was carried off. I felt for the lad, as I had experienced a dislocation of the knee and I realised his season was over. The tension was electric throughout a first half which saw a lot of goalmouth action but only one real shot on target by me which went past Ogden's left hand post. We had the better of the first half but went in level. In the second half I fired a great shot which hit Ogden on the nose (shades of Tommy Booth again?) and John Woodward blasted the rebound wide. The goalkeeper had to have extensive treatment to his face before he continued.

We managed to take the lead from a Barry Lyons indirect free kick. I had been fouled just outside the box on the left hand side. Barry took it and I got in front of my marker to head it back across goal into the far corner of the net. Next, Ian Butler used his magical left foot to crack a shot against the post but I headed the rebound over the bar.

The game became very tense and Oldham needed to get back into the game. Phil Burrows gave away a free kick in the 65th minute just outside the box and Maurice Whittle, who had a great left foot, curled the ball past Crawford into the top left hand corner of the net.

It was a tense finish and both sides were glad to share the honours and take a point each. For Oldham, the Whittle goal had nearly assured them of the title but we didn't care: a draw was good enough for us and we had achieved promotion.

For York City players and fans alike it was a dream come true. Out of the ashes of near relegation we had achieved the near impossible and climbed into the second tier of the English Football League.

The scenes on the pitch and in the stand were fantastic, and people were deliriously happy. For the players it was exciting to see so many fans beside themselves with joy completely immersing the ground in front of the main stand in maroon and white. Every player I talk to who played in that epic season remembers with a thrill and a shiver those scenes sent through them at Bootham Crescent that day. I will remember it as the greatest moment in my footballing life, thrilled that the goal I scored gave so much pleasure to so many loyal York City supporters and gave us players the chance to take on some of the major Clubs in the Football League's higher echelons.

The draw made it difficult for us to win the League and the euphoria of promotion ended in a damp squib at Halifax in mid-week and we lost 2-1. We went to Plymouth to finish our great season with a re-arranged match and won 2-0. The irony is that if we could have raised our game at Halifax we could have still won the League by a point. In the end it was Oldham who won the League with 62 points and Bristol Rovers held us off on goal difference with 61 points. What disappointed me was that the third team although getting promotion were not given a medal by the Football League.

Still, nobody can take the memories away from what was the greatest season in York City's history, or the memories of players and fans that turned up at Bootham Crescent that Saturday afternoon.

YORK CITY IN DIVISION TWO (CHAMPIONSHIP) 1974-1975

"Eboraci in alterum (patrocinium)"

For our success, we were given a Civic Reception at the Mansion House with Jack Wood, who was Mayor at the time. It was very low key considering the achievements and publicity we had brought to the City. We were disappointed, with no real acknowledgement from the Football League with regard to medals for our promotion and now a downbeat response from the Civic leaders and businesses of York. All of them gained either prestige or profit from what we did – and both, in a lot of cases.

The York City Directors tried to make up for what we considered a snub by taking us on a ten-day trip to Iceland to play friendly matches against local opposition. Under League rules at the time you could not take a team on holiday – a trip had to involve a match or training camp.

I think this was the first time York City had played outside of Great Britain. For the Geographers amongst us we arrived just over a year after a volcanic eruption on Heimaey just off the south coast of Iceland. Everybody was evacuated to the mainland and when we arrived Eldfell (Mountain of Fire) in Icelandic had become along with Surtsey (a new island formed in 1963 by offshore eruptions) the latest tourist attractions. It had formed in a volcanic eruption and created a major crisis for the island. Positives all over the country and Iceland were that it used heat from the cooling lava flows to provide hot water and generate electricity. The Players found it fascinating that there were hot baths available at no cost all over the cities and some outdoors – brrr! For Chris Topping and me it became a bit of a Geographical trip to keep us interested in the tour.

We won our first game in Reykjavik against Keflavik and beat them 4-2 and, typical of the Icelanders, it was a very physical game. Over 1,100 supporters watched that game in which Barry Swallow, Jimmy Seal, Dennis Wann and I scored the goals. We played our second game of the tour against Throttur-Valour in Keflavik and we won that game 3-1. I got the first goal and Jimmy Seal and Barry Swallow got the others. Over 700 watched the game, a good crowd for Iceland, and the Icelandic FA decided to arrange a third game against an Icelandic International Select team. Obviously the Tour was getting serious, and a victory against a new English Second Division side would be a scalp for them. We, on the other hand were used to unbeaten records, and this was going to carry on. I put us ahead after 25 minutes of the game and it was only late in the second half that John Stone sliced a clearance into his own net past Graeme Crawford to make the final score 1-1.

I came back from Iceland and Therese, Sheriden and I flew off to Malta for some sun and to recuperate from a hard but successful season – and definitely the best experiences of my footballing career to date.

THE 1974-75 SEASON BEGINS

We were back in training in early July to the bombshell that Phil Burrows, our left back and Player of the Year, had signed for Plymouth Argyle. This was a concern as it started to break up one of the best back fours I had played with. I wondered if Phil had thought it out. We knew the various altercations he'd had with Tom Johnston, but surely the opportunity of playing against Manchester United, Sunderland, Nottingham Forest and Aston Villa would have been tempting.

Well, the clash of personalities had to end and it was Phil who rushed out of the door at Bootham Crescent and York City lost its best ever left back. If he had only talked to me I could have advised him on a little less haste as I had done the same thing at Manchester City and found it tough at my next Club, Swindon Town, and regret my hurried exit to this day.

Pre-season started and we had a new left back in Peter Oliver and two new signings Micky Cave and Jim Hinch.

Keith Hunt came in for about five months as Commercial Manager in what was a turbulent time behind the scenes at York City. Keith was involved in us playing in shirts with a white Y front on them and an away strip of white with a maroon Y on them. I wonder who ended up with the original strip? In those days you were not allowed to keep your shirt, or exchange it; rumour has it that our old Chairman Michael Sinclair knows their whereabouts.

The same training regime we had used with great success in the last season was followed again and the pre-season passed with the players getting into shape. Micky Cave, a record £18,000 signing from Bournemouth, took John Woodward's place in midfield and Peter Oliver went into the team at left back for Phil Burrows, with Jim Hinch covering for Jimmy Seal and me as substitute.

However, there was always something bubbling just under the surface at York City, and past grievances were only kept under wraps by the players, and not forgotten.

Tom Johnston still kept in the background, managing the team from his office and well aware that the sale of Phil Burrows had not gone down to well within the squad. Something was bound to blow as the tensions mounted and we approached the biggest game in the Club's history against Aston Villa at Bootham Crescent.

Whether it was Keith Hunt's new ideas, or the new Chairman Bob Strachan and the Board or everybody getting carried away with the Club's elevation to the Second Division, I don't know. Something was being kept from us and we wanted to know what it was. The bombshell finally came the day before we played Aston Villa. After training Friday Tom emerged from his office and announced that there would be no car parking spaces available for the players and their wives on the ground. Instead we would have our pre-match meal at the Clifton Bridge Hotel; we would leave the cars there and walk to the ground.

Uproar, call it what you want, but we thought we had just become third class citizens, chucked on the muck-pile while the Directors played Big Time Operators without any consideration or discussions with us.

Another player's meeting. Tom Johnston and Colin Meldrum were asked to leave and the players slammed the door and another Bolshevik style meeting was in progress. After fifteen minutes of heated discussion, including some asinine ideas like refusing to play and not leaving the Clifton Bridge to go to the ground, we elected Barry Swallow and Barry Lyons as senior players to go and demand a meeting with the Chairman.

None of us thought that Tom would go out of his way and insist on car spaces for us, so it had to be the Chairman, Bob Strachan. When the lads came back we had been offered three nominated spaces in the car park for the season and designated cars would drive the 12 selected players to the ground. We accepted and duly arrived crammed like cattle into three of our cars for the match, but in the following weeks used the three spaces but parked the other cars in the nearby streets. Promotion to the Second Division had overawed the Directors and staff and they were too willing to look after the visitors at the team's expense. What a nonsense the day before a big game.

Well, the 17th August 1974 went down in Club history as our first game in Division Two (now the Championship) and saw us draw 1-1 with one of the giants of the game, Aston Villa. Barry Lyons scored our goal although I am sure a crowd of just under 10,000 fans disappointed the Board of Directors; maybe the fans couldn't get a car space close enough to the ground.

We were a close knit unit as a team, even though things seem to conspire against us as we prepared for the games ahead. The fans were still deliriously happy with what we were achieving on the pitch and a point in our first game gave all of us a lot of confidence.

We lost to Oxford United away 3-1 but I got my goal scoring season under way, crashing a right foot shot in off the underside of the crossbar. We then registered our first win in the Division 1-0 against Cardiff City at home and I was pleased to score that goal too.

Jimmy Seal got two against Notts County in a 2-2 draw at the Crescent and then we had a great win against Fulham 2-0 and I got both goals on London Weekend's *Big Match*. Bobby Moore and Alan Mullery were in Fulham's starting line-up and it was a windy day down at Craven Cottage making ball control difficult. We battled well in the first half and rode our luck a bit, with John Stone getting away with a hand ball close to the goal line which should have been a penalty.

Then Barry Lyons got the ball out on the right wing, advanced to level with the area before whipping in a cross to the near post and I got across my marker and side-footed it into the net for the opening goal. More pressure from Fulham until half-time, but we went in with a one goal lead.

It was more of the same in the second half but they didn't break us down. John Lacey, their centre back, decided on a pass back to Peter Mellor in goal but I anticipated it and beat him to the ball to slip it into the left hand corner and we were two up. More pressure, but we played on the counter-attack and I scored what I considered to be a perfectly good goal just before the end. I picked the ball up on the left hand side of the area and beat Mellor with a cross-shot, only to be pulled back for offside. It was a wonderful experience to play against England Internationals such as Alan Mullery and Bobby Moore. Bobby joined Fulham in 1974 for £25,000 from West Ham United. Fulham were in the second division and reached the FA Cup Final where they faced his old club West Ham United, but lost 2-0. This was Bobby's final appearance at Wembley as a player.

I found Bobby a quite unassuming player, a gentleman on the pitch, but with all the composure and know how to be in the right defensive positions at all times. I was lucky that John Lacey for Fulham did not have the same ability, or I would not have scored against them.

It was a really great start to the season, winning down in London against a fancied side who would later that season play in the Wembley Cup final against West Ham United. However the following week things turned out badly for the team and especially for our right back John Stone.

We were playing Sunderland, one of the teams fancied for promotion, at Bootham Crescent in front of an all ticket crowd of 15,000. John went into a tackle and came out with his ankle all awry. It was dislocated but it went back in, and then 24 hours later it came out that he had ruptured his Achilles tendon. Unfortunately he would be out for the season and that meant we had lost both our full backs inside a few months. It caused a fair bit of disruption and it was only at the end of December when Tom brought in young Cliff Calvert to fill the right back spot that we had a player giving consistently good performances. Brian Pollard would later join him in the team and get a good run until the end of the season. Brian would then move to Watford for a record £33,000 in 1976 and played under that legendary Chairman Elton John before a second spell at York between 1981 and 1983.

The end of September also brought an end to my run in the team when I dislocated my collar bone at Bristol City. Fearless or daft, I went for a diving header from a Barry Lyons cross and their goalkeeper Ray Cashley dived out and we collided. Ray, a bit heavier than me, came out OK but I was stretchered off and taken to Bristol infirmary for an x-ray.

Anybody who has had a shoulder displaced will know the agonising pain you feel and I was no different.

Well, the team coach picked me up at the hospital. I was pleased that the lads had managed to get a 0-0 draw but had to endure five hours on a coach with my left elbow propped on a skip. I had scored with a diving header against Southend the year before but on the way back from Bristol I vowed to take the diving header out of my repertoire. Brave or stupid – but I was to score other goals diving to head the ball, so that vow went out of the window.

I missed five weeks with that injury and the team during that time won three games and lost four before I took over again from Jim Hinch, who had only managed one goal as my deputy.

I came back to join up with Jimmy Seal again and we managed to win a couple more games, both of us scoring three goals including one goal each against Millwall at Bootham Crescent.

We lost 2-1 at Nottingham Forest on a very muddy pitch. Barry Lyons, back at his old Club, slung over a long cross beyond the far post and in in spite of my promise to myself, I dived in and scored, putting us back in the game. Paul Hince of Manchester City had it right when he said at Oldham Athletic in that Lancashire Senior Cup match, "You're bloody daft or mad, Jonesy, or probably both."

The team was working well again although we were having a few problems in defence but Barry Swallow and Chris Topping were still a formidable pairing as centre backs.

We had managed to reach sixth in the Division but during December we had a really bad run, losing to Southampton 2-1 away, Aston Villa 4-0, Manchester United 1-0 at home and Sunderland 2-0 at Roker Park.

The last three games were against really tough opposition and we did well to compete with the monied and talented squads they could put out against us.

Manchester United were top of the league and they were always going to return to the top flight, and it was another bumper crowd of over 15,000 in Bootham Crescent to see the encounter.

I always remember that the Manchester United supporters had a massive police escort from the railway station along Leeman Road and up and over Scarborough Bridge and along to the ground, and the same on the return trip. Stuart Pearson scored for Manchester United and I cannot say that it was a memorable match.

Roker Park on Boxing Day was a fiery encounter in front of 35,000 fans, with bad blood on both sides. There were altercations between Bob Stokoe and our captain Barry Swallow during the build-up to the game and in the papers, and there was a bust up between them in the tunnel after the game. Sunderland won 2-0 but it was a nasty affair both on and off the pitch and lived up to its "Boxing" Day billing. Bob Stokoe never forgot, and he carried that grudge on with me when he became Manager at Rochdale and managed to prematurely end my League football career.

We finished 1974 with a 3-0 home win against Hull City, Ian Holmes scoring two and Barry Swallow the third.

We joined the FA Cup in the Third Round as we were now a Second Division Club and drew Arsenal away at Highbury. John Woodward was pleased as Arsenal had been his first Club. In front of a 28,000 crowd we nearly pulled off the surprise of the round by leading Arsenal 1-0 with a Sealy spectacular from outside the box (I have to keep hearing from Jimmy about the goal and the one he scored at Old Trafford, even now, 40 odd years later).

The replay at Bootham Crescent was a close affair. It was 1-1 at full time with Barry Lyons scoring, but Brian Kidd who had scored in normal time added two more in extra time and the 15,500 crowd had seen a spectacular match and a near shock.

The Boss, Tom Johnston, left in January to go as General Manager to Huddersfield Town and it was a sad day for me. Tom had two promotion winning campaigns and managed York City in the highest Division they were to play in and for me that puts him down as the best Manager York City have had to date. Also he was one of the few managers who had real faith in my abilities to make a difference to a good side and score the goals necessary to take us into a higher Division, and for that I will be for ever grateful.

I felt at the time that the York City glory days could be coming to an end. Colin Meldrum had left, we had lost two of our stalwart defenders and Barry Swallow was starting to feel the wear and tear of league life. Barry Lyons and Ian Butler were at the wrong end of their careers and producing consistent performances was becoming harder. I realised that Jimmy Seal and myself were going to find it harder to score goals if our main supply was dwindling.

However, January became a productive month for us. Clive Baker took temporary charge and we drew against Southampton 1-1. I was shocked to find Clive put me in the reserves mid-week for a game at Chesterfield. But I was going through a lean spell and had not scored in seven games though my scoring partner Jimmy Seal had managed to get on the sheet. I duly played on the Wednesday night, scored a hat-trick and was back in the team at Norwich City who were one of the leading teams in the Division at that point in the season in third place and about to reach the League Cup Final. They lost the final to Aston Villa at Wembley but were to finish third in the Division and get promoted to the First Division.

Ted MacDougall and Phil Boyer, former York City favourites, were both in the Norwich City team and we won 3-2. This was probably our best performance of the season and it was needed as we had dropped to our lowest League position. We attacked down the right and a cross from Barry Lyons was not cleared and in the scramble in the six-yard box Sealy forced it in after just 83 seconds. Right away, Ian Holmes was down the right wing and he crossed into the box and I side-footed it into the net from 12 yards and we were two up inside two minutes. We held our lead until half-time with some good defending but the pressure was telling as we went into the second half hanging on.

They got a goal back to 2-1 with Colin Suggett scoring with a deflected shot before I put the game safe in the 75th minute as I drifted out to the right wing and picked up a pass from Barry Lyons and cut in from the touchline as the defence back-pedalled. I needed no second urging as I angled in on the right hand side of the area and cracked a rising shot past goalkeeper Kevin Keelan on the angle into the net off the underside of the crossbar to put us 3-1 up. They came at us again and got it back to 3-2 but we hung on for the two points and a very notable victory.

The match was televised so the Country knew that York City, the bookies' favourites to go straight back down, were no push-overs and likely to stay in the Division. I thought Clive Baker might keep the job as we only lost once in the next three games before Wilf McGuinness arrived. I had known Wilf while growing up at Manchester City. He was the Youth team Coach at Manchester United and had been one of the famous Busby Babes.

Wilf, like everybody else in Manchester United had the problem of managing George Best and his succession to the Manchester United post after Matt Busby was not easy. So Wilf joined York City from Greek Club Aris Salonika and he kept Clive Baker as his Coach. I helped Wilf to get off to a great start as Manager with a couple of goals at Millwall. The Den was a tough place to go to in those days with a fanatical East End of London following. I was careful where I celebrated those goals – definitely not close to Millwall supporters. Micky Cave scored our other goal in a 3-1 win.

Micky Cave went to America a few years later and was tragically killed in an accident in a garage in Pittsburg by carbon monoxide poisoning in November 1984. He was a quality player who helped York City stay in the Second Division for an extra season.

March 1975 was a tough month for the team and we knew we had to pick up some points to avoid being dragged into the relegation dog-fight. With seven games to go we knew that Sheffield Wednesday were adrift at the bottom of the League with 20 points but eight teams were within five points of each other. We needed to get a few wins before the end of March as we had to go to Old Trafford to play Manchester United who were run-away winners of the Division (they had gone down to a Denis Law goal against Manchester City at the same moment as I scored the goal that put York City into the Division Two in 1974).

Well, we lost away at Notts County in the first game 2-1 with Jimmy Seal getting our goal but managed to scramble a 1-0 win against Bristol City at Bootham Crescent, Brian Pollard scoring. But then we went down to Portsmouth and lost 1-0 at Fratton Park.

The gates during the season had dropped to below the 10,000 mark although the Club had put in seats in the Popular Stand in the Summer of 1974. I am sure that the seats were bought from the Platt Lane Stand at Manchester City which had increased the number of seats in the ground to 2,762. However this meant that the ground capacity was reduced from 20,000 to 13,000 spectators.

The Shippo where I scored the important goal to put us into Division Two had its capacity reduced to 5,105 and later after the tragic death of David Longhurst at that end reduced to 3,062 when The David Longhurst Stand was officially opened in October 1991 when we played Leeds United. A crowd of 4,374 saw that game which ended 2-2.

The game against Fulham was to determine our season and hopefully keep us out of the danger zone of relegation. By then Cardiff City had joined Sheffield Wednesday as the teams most likely to go down but it is a lot easier to decide your own fate and win the targetted games. Fulham, whom we had beaten at Craven Cottage on *The Big Match* in October were one of the sides we needed to beat.

The game became a five-goal thriller with York coming out on top 3-2. I always remember the Fulham games for pitting myself again the late great Bobby Moore, and for somehow coming out on top in the three games I played against him. Having scored the two goals at Craven Cottage I was about to get another two goals in the first 20 minutes of this match. Peter Mellor, the Fulham goalkeeper (whom I had played against when he was at Burnley and I at Manchester City in the Youth teams) must have dreaded playing against me as I always scored past him.

Brian Pollard, who was in for Barry Lyons on the right wing, whipped in a cross to the near post in the seventh minute and I made the run across two defenders and delicately clipped the ball with my right foot up and high over Peter and in off the far angle of the left hand post and crossbar.

Alan Slough equalised for Fulham after 11 minutes beating two of our players, Swallow and Calvert (after a pass from Les Barrett) and cracked a shot past Graeme Crawford. Unusually for us our defence didn't look too solid and it wasn't a surprise when Slough slipped past two of our players and crossed for Viv Busby (yes, the same Busby who formed the York City partnership with Denis Smith) and smashed the ball into the roof of the net after 19 minutes.

The game was just an attacking goalfest and the following minute Brian Pollard was off down the right wing again and fired a cross into the box and I again got across Bobby Moore and glanced a header across Mellor and into the net. The crowd was manic and baying for more goals as the game switched from end to end with chances going begging on both sides. I could have had a couple more goals with better finishing and the same went for Viv Busby for Fulham. Both sides got a standing ovation from the 7,500 crowd at half-time. We carried on in the attacking vein in the second half and after 50 minutes Ian Butler beat two men down the left wing and sent me through on goal. I raced down the middle and as I was in the process of shooting got clipped by Bobby Moore in the penalty area and, falling, blasted my shot wide. The ref pointed to the penalty spot and I wanted the goal to complete my hat-trick (I'd had that good goal disallowed earlier in the year at Craven Cottage which would have completed my hat-trick there).

Only Ian Holmes of our regular penalty takers was on the pitch as I put the ball on the spot but I could see Wilf McGuiness frantically jumping up and down as Ian ran up and shoved me out of the way. I looked over to the bench and Wilf looked a relieved man as I reluctantly relinquished the ball to Ian. Holmesy dutifully despatched the penalty (as he always did) and my immediate chance of a hat-trick disappeared. It was a great game to play in and chances went at both ends but none fell to me as the game finished 3-2, but it could have easily been 8-6. We all came off to a standing ovation and we knew that the points gave us breathing space at the bottom of the Division.

We had also completed the double over both the teams that would make Wembley appearances in the two major Cup Finals of 1975.

We were only to win one more game out of the last seven and that would be 3-1 away from home against Bristol Rovers, although we did manage to pick up draws against Blackpool 0-0, Bolton Wanderers 1-1 and Oldham Athletic 0-0 in the last game of the season.

From 7,500 fans at Bootham Crescent to see us beat Fulham to The Theatre of Dreams that was Old Trafford and Manchester United, and a crowd of nearly 47,000 on Easter Saturday hoping to see Manchester United go back to the First Division in style. Wilf McGuiness, back at the Club he had both coached, played for and managed, was in his element and it was a poignant day for him.

We walked onto the pitch 40 minutes before the kick-off and Wilf said, "Soak up the atmosphere, boys, it will be the best you ever play in. Listen to the Stretford End – they are already applauding us." We weren't impressed and Wilf said, "Let's go over there and applaud them back." We must have been daft but did as we were told and started to walk as a team to the Stretford End. The polite clapping as we approached the crowd suddenly slowed down to a slow hand clap and Wilf looked embarrassed as we got closer. By the time we got to the penalty area it changed into continuous booing, at which stage we beat a hasty retreat to the centre circle. At Old Trafford the tunnel is in the corner of the ground and as we went back in we had to endure another hostile booing session as we disappeared into the shelter of the away dressing room.

The game wasn't a spectacle and was more a game of defence. Like many sides that go to Old Trafford we were put under intense attacking pressure. York City were not any different on the day but in Graeme Crawford we had a goalkeeper on top form and he made a string of saves from Lou Macari, Willie Morgan and Steve Coppell. I had one chance with a header in the first half which glanced past Alex Stepney's left hand post but had to come off with a calf muscle strain at half-time when the score was 0-0 and Barry Lyons took my place.

It took until the 74th minute for them to break us down and then Willy Morgan managed to score and after 86 minutes our resistance was shattered with a second goal, from Lou Macari. My striking partner Jimmy Seal scored a goal for us after a goalmouth scramble in the 88th minute. This was the biggest league gate ever to watch York City in action, 46,802 beating the previous crowd of 40,000 at Hull City in 1949.

However we put in a gallant performance at Old Trafford and as it was a gala day for York City the Board of Directors put on a coach for the wives and girlfriends to go and watch the game.

Well, that left six games to go to secure safety in the Division and after Manchester United we lost 2-0 at Hull City and again I had to come off with the same leg injury. I was back for the following weeks to help secure a couple of draws at home against Blackpool 0-0 and Bolton Wanderers away at Burnden Park 1-1.

As always with York City teams through the ages we never made it easy for the fans and went and lost a home game to West Bromwich Albion 3-1 and the bookies shortened the odds on us going down. We were still a confident team at the time and knew we had enough fire-power to get some goals in our final games of the season.

It wasn't until the penultimate game at Bristol Rovers when we won 3-1 that safety was assured in the Division. The final game of the season was against Oldham Athletic at home and like the season before finished in a draw, this time 0-0, though without the tumultuous scenes which greeted the final whistle of 1974. Of the three teams promoted the season before, York City were to finish above both Bristol Rovers and Oldham Athletic in 1975 while Manchester United went back to the First Division as Champions.

I was fit again for the end of the season run-in and played in 37 games in our first year in the Second Division. My goal tally was 13 League goals and quite a good follow-up to the season before when I scored 17 League goals from 41 appearances. I think most League centre forwards of today would take that tally of 30 goals in 78 games at the level of Football York City were playing in between 1973 and 1975.

YORK CITY – THE LAST SEASON
1975-1976

Eboraci, in ultima tempore 1975-1976

The season came to an end and against all odds York City had not made a speedy return to the lower echelons of the Football League. Like the season before when we were given the no-hope tag for promotion, we had confounded all our critics by staying in the Division Two. The Board, after our Icelandic adventure of a close-season tour, decided to take us to warmer climes and arranged to go to Palma in Majorca. As the season before, we had to comply with League regulations to play a competitive game and arranged to take on Colchester United. However their side of the tour fell through and it was left to us to arrange a game against a Palma XI.

Wilf McGuiness was to call them "a bunch of Spanish waiters" and I had that ominous thought that the shades of Atlanta Chiefs might haunt me once again.

The game was played on a dusty pitch with a strong wind blowing and Graeme Crawford didn't want to bang-up his dodgy knee so we volunteered Ian Butler to play in goal. We had been at a big reception the previous night (just like Atlanta) and we were all a bit worse for wear. The game was to be played at mid-day in very warm weather. Wilf's team talk was brief: "Get them stuffed."

Buck with his 'Andy Capp' on his head (cartoon character from the sixties) and his 'bottle of water' (why was the water in brown bottles in Majorca at the time?) took his place in goal.

They kicked off and passed the ball back to the goalkeeper, who hoofed it downfield and a player hooked the ball on goalwards – an easy take for Buck – except he wasn't there. Feeling a bit dehydrated he was leaning on the post having a swig out of the bottle when the ball bounced past him into the far corner of the net. Wilf went ballistic and we sobered up pretty quickly after that and proceeded to take them apart. I stopped counting after seven but Wilf couldn't be appeased and ranted on about that goal for two days. It is a salutary lesson to always treat the opposition with respect, as the American tour had taught me.

By then it was time for Brian Pollard's birthday and the hotel had allowed the players and the Board to throw (why did I use that word?) a poolside party for Brian whose 21st birthday it was. Wilf by then had recovered and was back in his jovial mood, thank goodness.

Wilf had told the Board that he was pleased that his twin brother whom he had not seen for many years was flying in to Palma from Canada that evening. He was going to meet him and apologised for missing the start of the festivities but hoped he wouldn't be too long.

The party got under way without Wilf and was in full swing. We were all seated on one long trestle table, over 20 of us, with the Board all hovering at one end including the Chairman, Bob Strachan, and a good friend to this day, Dr Angus Mcleod.

The Boss was still missing when there was a kerfuffle at the door and a garrulous looking guy with a good set of hair, checked jacket, large kipper tie and a pair of Cuban heeled shoes Abba would have been proud of, tried to push his way into the party. Barry Swallow rushed over.. There was a great flourish of arms and gesticulations and he returned to the table to talk to Bob Strachan.

Barry told them that the guy was Wilf's brother and he was enquiring where Wilf was. Barry said he had explained that Wilf had gone to the airport to meet him..

Bob Strachan, as peacemaker, suggested that Barry should invite him over and join the celebrations and assure him Wilf would turn up soon. This seemed to appease Wilf's brother and he took a place near the Chairman. But when he spoke, his Canadian accent and his arrogance were calculated to cause offence. He started by wanting to be introduced to "Wilf's team" and then began to enquire insultingly about the players.

"Hey, who is that little fat guy, does he play?"

He was referring to Barry Lyons, one of our best players, but who was a bit stocky.

"Shouldn't he be a male model, he is so good looking?" pointing at Barry Swallow. Actually, Barry had done some modelling of clothes. He went on to enquire about most of the players, throwing out insults at us all. Finally he sat down, and went into conversation with the Directors who were excruciatingly nice to him. We got on with the party but kept eavesdropping on the odd comment as the Board started to shower compliments on the Boss in his absence. Wilf's brother seemed to lap it up as we kept making remarks about the whereabouts of Wilf – shouldn't he be back? In the end the staff wanted to bring in Polly's 21st birthday cake and make the toast.

In Wilf's absence Barry Swallow was asked to say a few words. He stood up and went to the Board end of the table to make his speech. He welcomed everybody to the party including Wilf's twin brother, thanked the hotel staff for the hospitality and the cake and asked everyone to be upstanding for the toast. "To Brian on his 21st birthday," said Barry and as he raised his glass swept the guy's wig off to reveal Wilf himself. We collapsed laughing, not quite believing that we had pulled off this spoof on the Board of Directors. Most of the Board looked mortified but the doctor, Angus McCloud, saw the funny side.

Everyone but the Board had been sworn to secrecy but none of us thought that the hoax could have played out for such a long time without somebody twigging it. Surely that light blue checked jacket I had worn to games must have been recognised, along with Cliff Calvert's colourful tie and that pair of Cuban heels? The wig, which nobody knew Wilf had until the tour, was the final touch to a perfect disguise. Everybody knew the Boss was almost bald and for somebody to appear like that was a great disguise – he should have been on the stage. Actually Wilf went on the after-dinner speaking circuit in later years and was excellent at the job of entertaining people.

I talked to Angus McCloud a few years ago and he thought Brian Pollard's 21st was a great night and, yes, he had been taken in by Wilf's disguise and accent. However Bob Strachan, a dour Scotsman, was not a happy Bunny and that night might have been plotting the beginning of the end of Wilf's tenure as Manager.

The party really got into full swing when the Board retired to bed and Wilf became himself again. He was hovering close to the poolside about midnight and pointing to something in the water, trying, I think, to lure somebody close to the edge. I was heading for the bar with a wad of Spanish notes in hand to buy a drink for the lads.

Anyway, Dennis Wann, a known prankster moved towards Wilf on the edge of the pool to have a look as we all crowded round. It was definitely Dennis Wann who nudged Wilf and he went into the water, Cuban heels, wig and all. I thought as I made my way to the bar that I had better pull him out but as I did so somebody pushed me in too. So about 4,000 pesetas in notes were in there, floating along with Wilf's wig which looked like a dead beaver. I had to kick my shoes off and was finally dragged out like a drowned rat. I looked at the pool again: there was the wig and all my money plus half of Polly's cake, a sunbed and a life-saving ring. Who chucked all that lot in?

I had my suspicions that Dennis had pushed me in after the Boss so 40 odd years later when I ran into him I confronted him with the question.

"Dennis," I said, "did you push me in the pool that night?"

He replied, tapping his nose: "Would I do a thing like that to you, Jonesy?" Well, I am still not sure, as all he did was tap his nose. What did that mean?

The birthday party ended for me as I retrieved all my money from the pool with a net and slopped off to my room to dry myself out and, more importantly, peg out the banknotes to dry on the line over the bath.

First off I had to check the room I was sharing with Topps to make sure Eric McMordie (one of Wilf's first signings) was not hiding in the wardrobe. We called him the Irish ferret, as he had the habit of moving from one room to another, apple-pieing your bed or jumping out of the wardrobe to surprise you. On this night all was clear and I was able to dry out and retire in comfort. My shoes I left on the bottom of the pool to be retrieved by the staff the following morning as I'd had enough water for one evening.

The rest of the tour was comparatively an anti-climax while some of us improved our tans on the beach and wandered round Palma while the rest of the lads managed to make it a profitable few days for the local tavernas.

Therese, Sheriden and me did our usual pilgrimage to Malta when we arrived back from Palma and when I returned to pre-season training the side which had taken us into Division Two had been decimated. Only Graeme Crawford, Chris Topping, Jimmy Seal, John Woodward and Ian Holmes would be contending for a place in the team at the end of the 1975-76 season. Wilf was putting his own team together and as results would prove, he did not make a good job of it.

However the season got under way with a win against Portsmouth with Barry Lyons and Eric McMordie scoring the goals. The spine of the team was still in place with Crawford in goal, Swallow and Topping at the back, John Woodward and Ian Holmes in the middle and Sealy and me still the strike partnership. Barry Lyons started the first eight games including three in the League Cup and then was discarded and Ian Butler, our other star wing man, had moved on. So the supply of ammunition had dried up and the movement and the know-how between us was no longer there, thus scoring goals became more difficult for Jimmy and me.

After the Portsmouth win, we lost in the first leg of the League Cup at Bradford City 2-0 and then lost in the League to Bristol Rovers away, our new full back Derek Downing scoring our only goal.

We played the second leg of our League Cup tie on the 26th August and produced one of our best performances of 1975, as it turned out. Being 2-0 down we went all out on attack and found the three goals necessary to progress in the Cup. Jimmy Seal got the first two goals and then I waded in with the third to win the match scoring past my old mate Peter Downsborough from Swindon days.

I scored my second goal in August away at Bolton Wanderers' ground Burnden Park. It was another nostalgic trip as I had frequented the ground as a youngster with my Uncle Bill back in the fifties when Nat Lofthouse was King of Burnden Park and thus I considered myself on hallowed turf. Unfortunately we lost 2-1 but at least my season was under way and the goal scoring partnership between Sealy and me was still active.

We were to play Liverpool in the League Cup on the 10th September but before that had to make a trip to West Bromwich Albion on the Saturday. I was happy about that as I had started to score goals again and this was to be my return to where I had scored my first goal in League Football for Manchester City.

Lingering in the back of all our minds was the continuing unease about the IRA and its mainland activities. The M62 coach bombing was still fresh in our minds and I believed the coach firms were on amber alert. I always thought that football teams and their dependence on coach travel to get around would be an easy target and a coup for the IRA.

Of course we were well aware of the Birmingham pub bombings which took place nine months earlier, killing 21 people. But you read it in the papers and it was "always someone else" and you carried on normally.

We travelled down to West Bromwich on the Saturday morning and stopped for our pre-match meal at the Post House in Great Barr. We then boarded our coach for the short trip to the Hawthorns when about a mile down the road we were suddenly surrounded by police cars and Army personnel. The police came on board and shouted, "Evacuate the bus as quickly as possible and get as far away from the area as possible. This is a bomb alert."

Wow! I have never seen a team get off a bus so quickly; women and children first did not come to mind at the time in the mad scramble to get clear.

We ended up walking to the ground and a little later we heard that it was a hoax and that our kit from the coach would arrive later after a thorough check. It didn't seem to affect our performance as we were to come out of the game with a creditable draw 2-2. Jimmy Seal and me were again on the score-sheet and were in confident move for the arrival of Liverpool in the League Cup the following Tuesday. The events on the Saturday hadn't affected the team but I again thought *there but for the grace of God go I.*

The game against Liverpool was played under floodlights in torrential rain and we were unlucky to lose. It looked as though we were going to hold the mighty Liverpool to a draw and go back to

Anfield when the ref gave a penalty in the last minute for a foul on Keegan by Topps. He gave the decision from way back from the action standing near me, 30 yards away, and must have done it on instinct. Anyway the penalty was despatched and Liverpool got away with it and won 1-0.

Maybe I should have sealed the game earlier as I had a chance to beat Ray Clemence, the England goalkeeper at the time, with a cross shot which went past his right hand post. Amazing, really, that over the seasons I played against the three best goalkeepers in English Football – Banks, Shilton and Clemence, and scored past two of them. I should have made Ray the third.

After that game we only managed one win, against Oxford United 3-1, and a creditable draw at Chelsea 0-0. From October we were to lose seven games on the trot and the bookies would not give you odds on York City staying in Division Two this time and it was only the middle of November.

A little light at the end of the tunnel came with our old friends Fulham coming to Bootham Crescent and we duly beat them 1-0. Again it was Bobby Moore with a late challenge on me in the box and again Ian Holmes put the ball in the back of the net. However the revival was short-lived and we lost the next three games against Bristol City 4-1 and Nottingham Forest away 1-0 (I was missing injured from both games) and a home Derby defeat to Hull City 2-1.

This game on the 20th December 1975 would be my last game for York City. although I was not to know it at the time. It was like the ten little Indians as the side of our glory days was dismembered, leaving by the end of December only Graeme Crawford, Chris Topping and John Woodward playing regularly in the first team.

By the end of December Barry Swallow would be out and Steve James would come in at centre half (a Manchester United player under Wilf). I had a hint from Wilf that I was going to be out of the side and he fancied Jim Hinch and Micky Cave as a strike partnership with Jimmy Seal playing left half or third striker. Ian Butler had left and Dennis Wann was tried on the left wing and the team was in a pickle.

For the first time in my career at York City I was dropped from the team although my goals per game ratio was still quite good considering the poor performances the team was putting in. I had scored four goals in the 17 League games and also scored in the League Cup as had Jimmy Seal in a struggling team. It looked like the Manager had got some response as York won two and drew two of the next four games. It was short-lived as they then lost another seven games before a mini-revival in late February and early March.

By then the season was over for me. Wilf had put me in the reserves over Christmas against my old nemesis, Sunderland at Roker Park. It was a night game and I was put through down the right side of the pitch and as I crossed the ball with my right foot the centre half Jack Ashcroft went into a slide tackle and was so late he would have been late for the next one as well. Anyway as my right foot went back to the turf his foot took me straight on the ankle and I watched with horror as my right ankle started to blow up like a balloon. How I needed the consolation of Sidney Rose from Manchester City at that moment, as I looked again at the ankle and thought once more that this was the end of my career. They took me off on a stretcher to hospital in Sunderland.

The specialist gave me the news that I had ruptured the ankle ligaments and thought it would probably have been better to have had a clean break. I was put straight into plaster and my leg never saw the light of day for six weeks. I saw Mr Hope, the specialist at the Purey Cust hospital in York, and he was none too hopeful as he finally took it out of plaster and had the leg x-rayed. Bad news: it had not healed properly and I spent another three weeks in plaster but luckily only from the knee-cap down, and after two weeks I was allowed to use a heel and put some weight on it. All this time I had to endure frustrations as I watched York City slip out of Division Two and I could do nothing to help save them.

I blamed Wilf McGuiness in a way, as he should have kept faith with the strike partnership which had put York City into the Division Two and kept them there against the odds. We were still scoring goals and with a better supply of ball I think Jimmy and me would have continued to do so.

However, we were from the team that Tom Johnston built, and I felt that Wilf, living in the shadow of a successful side, wanted to build his own team and Hinch and Cave were the men to do it around.

I managed to get back into training after extensive physiotherapy and a lot of work on a heel-board at home which strengthened the ankle. It still looked puffed up as I started to do some gentle jogging in straight lines. For confidence I had it strapped, but I was a long way from any sort of fitness.

It was the middle of March 1976 when I finally got rid of the plaster casts and the middle of April before I felt confident for anything but straight line running. The specialist had given me the OK that the ankle would be as good as new but I wasn't sure, as the season drew to a close. York City would finish with two home games and draw with Blackpool 1-1 and 2-2 with Chelsea.

The glory days had disappeared by then and the crowds dwindling as York City sank out of the Division Two and into the lower levels of the Football League. Since then York City have never reached those heights of the middle 70s again. I was a frustrated bystander watching this debacle at the time but was more than ever determined to get back into the side the following season and do my utmost to get us back up there amongst the big boys.

We again headed off with Therese and Sheriden to Malta to rest up but also to get the ankle into sea water and work to get it stronger for the following season.

I was feeling pretty fit when we reported for pre-season training and had no ill effects from my right ankle although I had kept it strapped for any training involving kicking and tackling. In Malta I had actually played for the Malta CID in a local game on Manoel Island and knew that after that outing on a dry and sandy pitch the ankle would stand up to the rigours of any competitive match.

Pre-season went very well but by then I knew that Jimmy Seal and I were not in Wilf McGuiness's long term plans. That was patently obvious when he paired Jim Hinch with Micky Cave as the strikers in the practise matches. Sealy was to get a couple of games with Hinch injured but the magic of what we had achieved as a striking duo was buried for ever by Wilf McGuiness.

I decided it was time to have a talk with Wilf about his plans and the future for me at York City. He was upbeat but flippant when he said, "Hinch and Cave played very well for us at the end of the season and I am playing them as a partnership this season."

I replied, saying, "That may be so but the teams you were turning out got the Club relegated. What are you expecting Jimmy and me to do?"

Still flippant, he said, "Well I want to transfer one of you and the other I will keep as back-up in case of injury or loss of form."

I asked, "Are there clubs interested in signing us or will you let us have a free transfer?" I knew that no way was the Club going to allow us to go for nothing – I thought the Club could only get money for about six of the squad and that Jimmy and me were two of the major assets.

Wilf replied, "As a matter of fact your old Boss Tom Johnston wants to sign you for Huddersfield Town – do you want to talk to him?"

I said, "It looks like you have already set this up and if I am not wanted I will have a word with Tom."

As in the past I was to make a hurried decision to get away from a Manager who did not want me. I should have taken my own advice and given a lot of thought to the move as Wilf was heading into trouble with the York City team, and in time I am sure I would have got back into the line-up. I should have realised that he needed money to strengthen his side and to do that he had to sell, and I was one of the few he could get a fee for. I thought I was lucky getting out of the door first and signing for Huddersfield Town and my old Manager, but the move proved to be a nightmare as things were not at all well at Huddersfield Town.

I had a talk with Tom and he knew about my ruptured ankle ligament problem but he said that Huddersfield Town would take the risk if the x-ray was all right. I said I would sign if the terms were right and the x-ray was OK. Everything seemed to go smoothly as a fee was agreed, my signing on fee and salary were acceptable and I was going to be allowed to stay in York and travel over to Huddersfield.

Just as I was putting pen to paper Huddersfield demanded another x-ray and a specialist's report. I nearly backed out of the deal at the time and wish I had as things were about to go pear-shaped. I also knew that Grimsby Town were interested in Jimmy Seal and I thought if Jim goes first I would be resigned to reserve-team football, something I could ill afford at this stage in my career. The second x-ray was all right and two days later I went over to Huddersfield and signed. My time at my second City was over and I hoped a new goal scoring chapter would open with my old Manager Tom Johnston.

A FOOTBALLING NOMAD 1976-1980

On arrival at Huddersfield Tom introduced me to the Coach John Haselden whose first words to me were, "If it had been me I wouldn't have signed you, we have enough centre forwards on the books". This guy had no personality whatsoever and somehow I had to get along with him. A Colin Meldrum he was not, and I decided to confront Tom Johnston with this situation. He admitted that as General Manager he had forced the deal through and that there was some animosity at the Club about signing me. He said that while he was there things should be OK as he puffed on that pipe of his. Haselden had to go along with this and I was in the team for 12, games scoring two goals, before the bombshell dropped that Tom had been relieved of team duties and Haselden was taking over.

I went up to see Tom Johnston in his office at the time and all he said was, "I am sorry this has happened to you but you are on your own now and Haselden doesn't like you and probably won't play you."

I said to Tom, "Is it possible you can get me away from here as I don't want to stay where I am not wanted?"

"Sorry Son," said Tom, "but my hands are tied."

This was to become my worst nightmare as Tom Johnston was shunted to the sidelines, shortly to leave the Club, leaving me stuck with Haselden for three months. It was difficult to converse with a man who completely dislikes you and I couldn't understand why. However, I was a hardened professional by that time and was going to fight my corner and try to change his mind. His first team sheet had me absent and I was not even in the reserves. For two months this non-personality man had me coming over for training daily and not playing in a competitive match. I didn't know I could hate somebody so much and it came to a head just after Christmas. Fred Ford, my Manager from the Swindon days, was at Oxford United and had heard of my predicament and wanted to sign me. He knew the reserves had a mid-week game at Wolverhampton Wanderers and wanted to run the rule over me before making an offer.

At last, a glimmer of hope, as I went to see Haselden and asked him to put me in the team at Wolves as this was a chance for him to get rid of me – and me of him. I was flabbergasted when he said he had picked a team for the game and I was not in it. I waded into him then and told him what a shit he was and that he was acting like a little Hitler. I said I would go above him to the Directors. Fred Ford duly turned up at that game and was disappointed I was not playing. I phoned Fred the next day to apologise and he was amazed at the attitude of somebody who was running a Football Club but said unless I was playing and he could run the rule over my form he couldn't sign me.

The Club had paid money for me and they were reluctant to let me go at that stage. I pleaded my case that if the Manager was not going to play me then I would not be an asset to the Club much longer. What they thought of the man they appointed after Tom I don't know, but I knew he was clueless and daggers were drawn as he made me suffer.

In April 1977 I was put out of my misery when I managed to get my contract paid up with a mutual understanding between me and the Board. As I left the ground at Leeds Road I gave the two fingers' to Haselden but he was so docile he didn't even respond to me. To this day I cannot even put him in my category of Bad Managers as he was a nothing person to me.

I will always be thankful to Stan Anderson, the Manager at Doncaster Rovers back in 1977, who offered me a contract to play for him. Stan captained all the big North East clubs, Newcastle, Sunderland and Middlesbrough. He was a quality coach and manager, who always preached possession of the football. With me being a free agent, the PFA were in constant touch with me and Gordon Taylor, now working at the PFA, helped out. I knew him from his days at Bolton Wanderers with Brian Bromley. We had taken our coaching badges at the same time at Maine Road and the PFA asked me to play in Alex Dawson's (Doncaster Rovers' centre forward) testimonial match at Frickley Athletic's ground in South Elmsall.

I jumped at the chance for a game and amongst a fair number of professionals, including Stan Anderson, managed to score a hat-trick. After the game Stan said to me that if he sold Peter Kitchen in the close-season to Orient he would like to sign me in his place. I accepted the offer but said if somebody else wanted to talk to me I would have to listen and maybe go somewhere else. Stan Anderson was true to his word: Peter Kitchen went to Orient and Stan signed me for Doncaster Rovers. I will be forever grateful to Stan for resurrecting my career after that complete nightmare at Huddersfield Town and I hoped I could repay him with some goals for my new Club.

The 1977-78 season got off to a reasonable start for me although I did not manage to score as many goals as I would have liked. Stan was a fair Manager and had Cyril Knowles of Tottenham Hotspur as Coach. I played in over 20 games for Rovers but only managed four goals by mid-February 1978; I did not manage to ignite the team and was having to play in the position the local hero Peter Kitchen had played. So everything I did was measured up against him and I fell short in the supporters' minds. However I was still living in York and travelling into Doncaster by train, which was no hardship.

Towards the end of January 1978 Stan asked me to go out on loan to Darlington to get some match practise. Peter Madden the Manager wanted me to link up with Jimmy Seal, Dennis Wann and Barry Lyons again and try to help them avoid having to apply for re-election to the Football League. As I was only on the bench at the time I agreed to go to Darlington and found that all the York lads were travelling up to Darlington together. So again, no hardship: we car-shared and the attacking links were back in place, although we were all that bit longer in the tooth.

I managed only three goals in 16 appearances in the back part of the season but the goals were vital to Darlington and the third goal I scored preserved their position in the League and so they did not have to apply for re-election.

The start of the 1978 -79 season saw me back at Doncaster Rovers although I was hoping to have stayed and played at Darlington. But

Stan Anderson wanted me back and so I started the season there but like a lot of Manager's he found himself under early pressure from his Board of Directors.

I was still at Doncaster when Stan lost his job and Billy Bremner took over. I formed a partnership for a game with none other than Bobby Owen who was indirectly the reason for me leaving Manchester City in the first place. Events had been happening fast at other clubs and Peter Madden was no longer at Darlington but had gone to take charge of the bottom Club in the Football League, Rochdale.

At the time Rochdale had been seeking re-election regularly from the Football League and it was only their legendary Chairman Fred Ratcliffe's influence which stopped them going into the non-League wilderness. It was rumoured that if Rochdale finished in the bottom four at the end of 1978-79 season they would be goners.

Disaster had struck Rochdale in the FA Cup when they lost to non-league Droylsden 1-0. Billy asked me to go and talk to Rochdale with a view to going out on loan and possibly a permanent signing. When I arrived at the ground in December 1978 the place was like a morgue and it felt like one of those ghost towns with tumbleweed blowing through it. I had to wander in through a gate the groundsman had left open and followed it to the player's tunnel, with still nobody in sight.

Peter Madden appeared and ushered me into his office. I asked him where the players were and he said they were in the other changing room, feeling down at the moment after the FA Cup defeat to non-league opposition. However he said that wasn't going to be the picture much longer and that with my help and three new signings we could turn the Club around. I knew that Bobby Hoy was signing from my old Club York City and Brian Taylor from Doncaster was going to join too and this gave me a bit of a lift as we were signing good quality professionals.

Just as with Tom Johnston at York I was concerned about the onus being put on me to score the goals. Rochdale at the time were well adrift of the clubs above them including Halifax Town, Darlington Crewe and Northampton Town and it would take a monumental effort from then until the end of the season just to stop being the foot rest for the Football League. The spectre of finishing in the last four and the virtual certainty of going out of the Football League did nothing to raise the gloom as I worriedly signed a loan deal with Rochdale.

This, I could see, was going to be one of the biggest challenges of my career but I had seen Peter Madden work at Darlington and had faith that the right footballing things would happen at the Club. Peter, like Malcolm Allison and Fred Ford, was a big man with a personality to match and, like them, would not suffer fools gladly. We were lucky that the weather was atrocious during December 1978 with many games put off because of snow and the Pools Panel meeting to decide the result of games. Peter had the chance to get the players working together without playing a League game. We went and played a friendly at Bolton Wanderers and won 4-0 and I scored a couple of goals and thought at the time that this was not a bad set of lads and if we could pull together we might get some wins under our belts.

On the 30th December 1978 we got off to a great start by going over to Scunthorpe and shocked the footballing world by winning 4-0. The pitch was covered in snow, partly frost-bound the blizzard conditions really made the game a farce. Like the Manchester City game of the sixties against Tottenham Hotspur it was like a ballet on ice' but probably with not as much skill. It would never have been thought to start the game in the modern era but we got on with it and very glad we did.

We played a very direct game in those conditions and I scored after 20 minutes from a through ball and I drew out my old mate Graeme Crawford and scored with a low right foot shot. Bobby Hoy added a second before half-time. There were two more goals in the second half from Bobby Hoy and Terry Owen to win our first away game of the season. *Sports Report* at five o'clock when giving out the Football League Division Four results said, "I will repeat that score, Scunthorpe Nil Rochdale Four," as if in disbelief.

But the team did have its belief back and although we didn't go on a long unbeaten run we won enough matches to give ourselves a chance of getting out of the bottom four, considering we didn't play a home game in three months during that season due to the atrocious weather conditions in Rochdale (I still think that record stands). In January 1979 Doug Collins took over as Manager (much to our dismay as we were playing for Peter Madden) and we went down to Portsmouth and drew 1-1.

On 3rd February 1979 we had to go to table-toppers Wimbledon and Doug Collins was now in joint charge with Peter Madden. We shocked the League leaders by going two goals up only to be pegged back and Wimbledon finally came out on top 3-2.

On the 3rd March 1979 we had to go to Darlington to play what was a four pointer as Darlington were in as much trouble as we were. David Esser scored one goal and I scored a spectacular second, volleying past goalkeeper Burleigh to win 2-0 and we still had our sights on getting out of the bottom four. On March 11th the conditions at Spotland relented and we finally managed a home game against Hartlepool United who was just above us in the League and we drew 1-1. We then had a horrific loss to Grimsby Town 5-2 and although I scored in the first minute of the game and Eric Snookes got a second we were well and truly turned over by a side who were already heading for promotion to Division Three.

By the time we came to the start of May 1979 we had managed to haul ourselves up to second bottom of the Football League but we had games in hand. Doncaster Rovers were four points ahead but they had finished their season with a 4-3 win at Grimsby and Darlington were still struggling. We still had four games to play and hammered Northampton Town 4-1 at Spotland and I managed to score two goals in that game. I always knew that it was a ground where I could score from that game in the Lancashire League 15 years previously when I scored for Manchester City A.

We still had two games left to find three points for the safety of fifth place from the bottom and by the last game needed to go to Crewe and win to assure us of not having to apply for re-election.

We won 2-1 in an electrifying atmosphere at Gresty Road with me getting the first goal, a header from a Bobby Hoy cross which I put past the Crewe keeper Kevin Rafferty. Mark Hilditch got the important second goal, again from a header from Bobby Hoy's cross. Against all the odds we had got Rochdale out of a spell in the Northern Premier

League, retaining their Football League status for another year. In 1980 they would again have to apply for re-election but stayed up by one vote from my old Club Altrincham.

THE WINTER OF DISCONTENT 1979-80

Hiems tristitia finis footballing Odyssea.

Historians will know that the Winter of Discontent to be the year of 1978-79 but in Rochdale's case it came a year later when Bob Stokoe arrived and the cry of "Crisis, what Crisis?" was heard throughout the Club.

The season started all right in August 1979 with Doug Collins continuing as Player-Manager with Peter Madden still controlling things on the training ground and from the dugout. My move from Doncaster Rovers had been made permanent in the Summer.

The first game of the season was on 11th August 1979 when we travelled to Blackpool in the League Cup and drew 1-1. I scored from a header in the 43rd minute from an Eric Snookes cross and got my own personal season off to a flier. Denis Wann (the prankster from York City days), who had joined Rochdale from Darlington, got himself sent off and we couldn't hang on to the win as Blackpool equalised late in the second half.

We lost 1-0 in the replay at Spotland and after the game I noticed an old adversary, Bob Stokoe, near the players' dressing room. I saw him again at the next home games against Bournemouth, Hartlepool (when I scored the only goal of the game after half an hour from 25 yards, the ball skidding into the net) and Walsall and said to Dennis Wann, "He is hovering like a vulture waiting for Doug Collins to fail, if he is not on a scouting mission for some club."

By the end of September I had managed to score three goals in nine appearances but with nothing forthcoming from other players we had slumped to next to the bottom of the Division.

On 6th October 1979 I made my final appearance at one of my spiritual homes, Bootham Crescent. It was a nostalgic day for me as I realised that the chances of playing on that ground again were diminishing.

It was to be a memorable match for me as I scored and York City won 3-2. We were a goal up in 13 minutes from John McDermott who beat Joe Neenan for his debut goal. Peter Lorimer (whom I had the privilege of playing with in the Leeds Past Players' side for many years) and Joe both disputed the goal and Joe got booked. We won a corner on the left wing and as the ball fell out to me I scored with a shot which went in off Joe's left hand post a collector's item for me although I don't think the York supporters saw it as such at the time.

Terry Eccles got a goal back just before half-time and York fans who go back that far will remember the equaliser from John Byrne (what did Byrney do after that)? The winning goal for York came in the 86th minute from Barry Wellings who headed in a free kick from Peter Lorimer, putting it into the top left hand corner of the net.

On a Friday 26th October I was to score my last hat-trick in the League, against Northampton Town. We won 3-2 and I still have the autographed match ball (red and white leather panels). Northampton Town was a side who I could always score against having put two past them the season before in a 4-1 win. We had to come from behind twice in this game and my goals came in the 45th and 68th minutes with the winner five minutes from the end. I was announced as Man of the Match and at the final whistle grabbed the match ball from the ref, Pat Partridge. I have a lot of good memories from the game and playing for Rochdale even though the end was going to be catastrophic.

Bob Stokoe was in the crowd that night and Doug Collins knew that his job was on the line. I and the team had saved him for a few weeks longer but the Sword of Damocles was well and truly hovering over him. It fell three weeks later after defeats to Wigan and Bournemouth and a draw with Hereford.

Lo and behold, into the Club came my old Nemesis Bob Stokoe to be "the saviour" of Rochdale. His first match was an FA Cup game against Scunthorpe and I was surprisingly in the side. Jimmy Seal had joined us, probably on the recommendation of Peter Madden who had us together for some games at Darlington, and with Mark Hilditch we had three strikers on the pitch. Brian Hart scored our first goal before Pilling got an equaliser. Just before half-time I got the winner with a header which put Bob Stokoe on his pet dream – a run in the FA Cup – and, of all people, it was me who set it up for him.

Bob Stokoe had a grudge against some of us York City players after our matches in the 1973-74 season and the bad blood was still around from the John Stone incident and tackle at York City, and the Boxing Day flare up in the tunnel at Roker Park.

I only played one more match after that win against Scunthorpe and found myself warming the bench for the rest of December 1979 and January 1980. During that time we stayed slumped on the bottom of the Division Four and, horror of horrors, went out of the FA Cup to Bury in a replay 3-2.

We had lost a game at Tranmere 5-1 and Stokoe blamed the players for not trying and wanted to stop the players' wages. I wasn't even on the bench for that match but was in the stand and saw Tranmere put in a hard-working performance but on this particular night it just didn't go for the Rochdale lads and they got hammered. It was like Brazil's against Germany in the World Cup in 2014, though I am sure they didn't have a threat to their wages.

Bob Scaife, who was our PFA representative, had to fight to stop Stokoe carrying out his threat of fines, and on appeal he had to back down. We had threatened strike action and Stokoe, the Vice Chairman and Bob had to attend a Football League Appeals Committee at Lytham St Annes and give evidence on the Club's right to fine players under breach of contract.

The Club had to withdraw their case after evidence that lasted 90 minutes: Bob Scaife rightly said that the players had given 100 per cent at Tranmere Rovers – it was just one of those nights where things would not go right for the team. A back-handed slap by Stokoe said, "I can live with my conscience and hope the players can live with theirs after this." Cliff Lloyd, the Secretary of the Professional Footballers' Association, and my old friend from better times, Gordon Taylor, who was Chairman of the PFA, was pleased with the outcome and a strike by the players was avoided.

At the end of the hearing Stokoe had the last word and it was a chilling one for players at Rochdale when he said, "I only hope Cliff Lloyd will show the same consideration for players if we finish in the bottom four, fail to get re-elected and finish in the dole queue." In Bob Stokoe's character at the time the glass was not only half empty but I think there were only a few dregs left in it, if that.

He then brought the BBC in to interview him and put his case through the media and asked a couple of the players to state their case. It turned out to be quite embarrassing, listening to him say that professionals at the Club were not trying. I, along with the rest of the squad, felt insulted at his attitude and to me in particular who had given my game everything in the 17 seasons I had been playing and I was not going to stand for it.

One of his complaints was that the strikers were not scoring goals and I could hear him say: "Ask them, maybe they can tell you why we are not scoring." So the interviewer put the question to Mark Hilditch and then Jimmy Seal but they buckled in front of the cameras.

I don't think Bob Stokoe expected them to ask me as I was out of the side at the time. Same question.

"Chris, why have you not been scoring goals?"

My reply was, "I have scored seven goals in the 16 games I played until the end of November."

"Well that is a good ratio until then, but what since?"

I don't think the interviewer expected the answer I gave him.

Pointing at Stokoe I said: "You better ask him over there – even I find it difficult scoring from the fucking bench." End of interview, obviously not used by the BBC as it didn't fit the programme slant and the language was obviously unacceptable.

After that I knew I would be lucky if I lasted until the end of the season.

That brought me to that musing thought of the Winter of Discontent and all its frustrations culminating on that outburst in front of the television cameras. Shakespeare's opening quote from Richard III is:

Now is the winter of our discontent
Made glorious summer by this son of York...

Quite appropriate, I thought at the time, but summer would find me back at York and looking for another Club as Stokoe would gain his revenge on the team that he thought had embarrassed him.

I was back in the side after that, probably with Peter Madden's backing, he admired my stance against what I thought was injustice from Stokoe. I think any hope of escaping from the Football League basement was fading fast. Bob Stokoe could not transfer the FA Cup magic of 1971 at Sunderland to League form at Rochdale.

We lost my first game back in the team 3-0 at Portsmouth but without luck and in our next game at home to Doncaster Rovers on the 12th February we again played well this time winning 3-1. Again I was on the score sheet against one of my old Clubs and relished showing Rovers what they had missed two seasons before. Steve Lister had put them ahead but Brian Taylor equalised with a header from a cross from Nigel O'Loughlin. I then scored a couple of goals, one running on to a through ball and beating Denis Peacock in goal with a low shot and then lobbing him from outside the box as he advanced for my second. We won the game 3-1, but I never heard a "well done" from Stokoe whose pessimistic attitude to what was happening at Rochdale made me feel that he should have gone and left Peter Madden in charge.

That was not to be, as we all stuck the season out to the bitter end. I finished as leading scorer with 12 goals and the Supporters' Player of the Year trophy at the last game of the season.

We won two games in a week beating Newport County and finishing with a revenge win over Tranmere Rovers 2-0. Mark Hilditch scored in the 67th minute after goalkeeper Dickie Johnson had only managed to fist a shot from me back to Mark and he made no mistake from six yards out. The *Daily Mirror* reported: *Player of the Season Chris Jones settled matters with five minutes to go when he headed a cross in from the right wing.* However being bottom of the League and having to seek re-election was a bitter pill to swallow for all of us.

It was not the *Daily Mirror* but Stokoe who settled matters and took his revenge by advising the Board not to keep most of the players. After my past altercations with Stokoe and the fact that we couldn't stand one another I was top of his list for a free transfer. *Match Weekly* in January 1980 had me in the top 60 players in the Country for total number of games played to the number of goals scored, at an average of 3.03 with the likes of Peter Osgood of Chelsea and Peter Withe of Aston Villa below me in the chart. You would have thought that somebody who could score at an average of one goal in every three games throughout a poor season would have been an asset to Rochdale. But I was glad to be going, though very soon Stokoe left saying that he didn't think the players he released should play for the Club again.

Bob Scaife was another casualty and I felt it was an injustice that somebody who had represented us at the PFA hearing should have left probably because of the spite of the Manager. All told, Hitler's Night of the Long Knives in 1934 looked like a kids' game alongside this massacre as the Club got rid of 14 players from the staff of 20, leaving Peter Madden, who had built most of the team, in the lurch. Jimmy Seal and Dennis Wann from better days at York City were also kicked onto the scrap heap.

Once I knew Stokoe had left Rochdale I phoned Peter Madden to see if he wanted me back, as goal scorers at the time were at a premium. However, Vice Chairman, Mr Wrigley would not agree to resign players Stokoe had released. Even though the PFA had ruled it illegal to withhold player's wages. I am sure the fans would have liked me back also but the poison Stokoe had spread made the situation difficult for all parties. The Board backed Stokoes parting shots and Peter wasn't going to lose his job on a principle of bringing his leading scorer back and I was sacrificed.

The PFA helped players to find other clubs and I ended up going across to Le Havre Football Club in France and spent the summer there. However it did not work out for me and I realised I couldn't settle, so I returned to the UK but unfortunately was not taken on by a League club.

So my footballing odyssey ended at Rochdale and like most footballers at the end of their career had to find other work. We opened a small Hotel in York and I took a degree in teaching. Life after football moved on, although I kept in contact with many footballers and had an enjoyable time playing in charity games, raising money for the Leeds Infirmary with the former Leeds United players for many years.

These charity games became quite a lifeline for me as I looked to enjoy football at a high level with quality players such as Peter Lorimer, Eddy Gray, Bobby Collins, Terry Yorath and Billy Bremner, not to forget the great John Charles. I was always indebted to the late Ron Mollatt who played 125 games for York City between 1955 and 1960 for introducing me to the Leeds United players and giving me a new lease of life in football for many years. John Charles used to joke that as I was an 'outsider' (not having played for Leeds United) I was on a weekly contract and had to keep playing for my place in the Charity team.

They were wonderful players and characters at Leeds United and a credit to Don Revie who in most cases they had played under. It was a career away from the time of the Youth team quarter-final match between Manchester City and Leeds United at Elland Road in 1964 in which I had played and scored. It still gives me wonderful memories of a time passed before the formation of the Premier League in 1992.

THE PREMIER LEAGUE

In 1990 Liverpool, Everton, Manchester United, Tottenham and Arsenal had formed a secret coalition to try and break away from the other Divisions and form a Premier League

The administrative rivalries between the Football Association and the Football League were going to be a stumbling block. They argued over commercial rights, the Club versus Country controversy and players' wages.

I remember the late Billy Bremner of Leeds United voicing his opinion that it was a disgrace that a player's match fee for playing in a Cup final in the 70s at Wembley was a measly £100. He argued that if Frank Sinatra had played Wembley Stadium he would have commanded a minimum £100,000 fee.

His complaint was scoffed at by the Football Association who at the time was making millions out of the game and to their detriment putting very little back into the game from grass roots up.

Although Billy was ridiculed for his statement (the common idea was that it was a professional's privilege to play at Wembley in front of 100,000 "adoring" fans).

This was far from the way of thinking by professional footballers and deep down resentment was rife at the differentiation between footballer's wages and the Association's millions.

It was only in 1961 that the maximum wage was removed after Jimmy Hill, the Chairman of the Professional Footballers' Association had led a strong campaign on behalf of the players. Johnny Haynes of Fulham became the first £100 player in the Football League.

Thirty years later Noel White and David Dein, Vice-Chairman of Arsenal, were deputed by the five leading clubs to approach the

Football Association. The clubs in question were Everton, Liverpool, Manchester United, Arsenal and Tottenham Hotspur.

The Football Association succumbed. Instead of assessing the financial state of the game and realising the problems and disasters of the 1980s was behind them, they listened to the delegation from the Football League and sold football's soul to mammon.

Thus a veritable Pandora's Box was opened and in 1992 the Premier League was formed as the top 22 clubs broke away from the Football League in order to increase their incomes and make themselves more competitive in Europe. By selling TV rights separately the clubs increased their income and exposure. The rich then got richer and the poor League clubs got poorer and were left to fend for themselves with the scraps from the masters table.

The days of the professional footballer being in the grip of the clubs with a one year contract and a year's option to renew in favour of the clubs had gone. In came the player with his agents, the lure of wealth bringing the best players from foreign countries into the League.

A helter-skelter of good young home grown players dropping into the lower Divisions became the norm as they searched for first team football.

Ipso Facto the English and the Home Countries International sides deteriorated and it will be many years before a 1966 team to excite the nation comes round again.

My old Club Manchester City provides the prime example, when a few years ago they signed Yaya Toure for a wage said to be £221,000 a week plus bonuses and Champions League qualification money, to say nothing of "image rights", whatever that means – a total of £11 million a year besides the £24 million they paid to Barcelona.

During the last global financial crisis a lot of people got quite rightly angry about the amount of money bankers earned. We had a moral outcry and people were up in arms and asking the Government to step in.

But it seems that football lives in a kind of alternative world, cut off from the realities of society, cuts in services, banking meltdown and everybody having to belt-tighten.

In Football it now seems that the sky is the limit.

When we heard that Bryan Robson of Manchester United was being paid £1,000 a week in 1981 there was outrage and people chanted "what a waste of money" at him. Now nobody even blinks at what the players are earning although they might still shout "what a waste of money".

Wayne Rooney is the latest player to follow the likes of Yaya Toure and is earning over £300,000 a week. There are two possible reactions to this, one is to shrug your shoulders and just say "that's how the market works". The other is that football has gone completely bonkers and nobody is doing anything to stop the madness.

Football has no wage cap, unlike the wealthiest sports in the United States. Here clubs can pay what they like, buy whom they please and sell who they like. In Italy they have a name for this; it is called financial doping.

It seems to me that it is the fans as always who are the dopes who are having to pay for the excesses.

But the wages of Toure at Manchester City and Rooney at Manchester United as examples pose a moral dilemma for all of us who love the game. How can such excess ever be justified in the name of football?

Should we not all feel just a little bit ashamed to go and watch football as jobs are lost to foreign competition, schools and hospitals struggle or are closed down and students are denied university places?

Yet there is very little we can do about this football madness. Even if every fan in the UK stopped buying season tickets or stopped watching Sky this would have no effect on Manchester City's finances and a few more clubs which are totally unconnected with the sport, or its supporters. The Premier League's bloated football stars have all been over-rated but their wages will remain at their current absurd levels.

The game booms and "the product", backed by mass media coverage, has taken on a whole new image. Foreign players have flocked to the cash cow which is the Premiership. The game has been taken away from a lot of supporters who found going through the turnstiles with, say, a couple of youngsters too expensive. Still, there is always the TV channels with the big games and mass advertising to keep the supporters happy.

Like every product sold through mass media, brilliant though it is portrayed it has its flaws and usually it is the supporter who suffers in his pocket.

Football clubs trying to keep up with the pace of change and having to find money they do not really have brings casualties, and probably in the next decade some of our most loved Football League clubs will disappear into oblivion.

Football as it once was is dead, but the show goes on and on and on.

The grass roots of the game where my story started back in the fifties will just be a distant memory.

THE PARK REVISITED

"parcum visitasti"

My story started in the park as a young boy and I feel I should finish this narrative at the same place. But not in Stamford Park where I started but any park in any part of the Country where a young boy might be playing football with his dad or uncle and dreaming the dream of becoming a professional footballer. The time now, though, is the present, not nearly 60 years ago when I dreamed my dream.

The question I now ask is: has grassroots football changed in all that time? Is it any easier now for a young boy kicking a football about in the park to realise his dreams and aspirations? Have we moved on and improved things for youngsters at the start of their football dreams or are they still stagnated at the base of the football pyramid?

I believe that we have not gone forward in the growing of young English talent and I still question the coaching structures we employ for development.

The simplicity of the Football Association and the Football League has now been complicated by the formation of the Premier League (see my postscript at the end of the book) and the breakaway clubs in 1992.

Funding bodies like Sport England threaten The Football Association with the reduction of funding to grassroots football and there is greed and avarice involved in capturing young talent. Clubs approach the parents of a boy as young as age nine, just because he seems to have above average ability to play football. The parents see a glittering future for their youngster having watched the footballing superstars on TV and accept a bung for a signature to tie the youngster to a particular club in the hope that he makes the grade.

If the young home growth youth player makes it through the academy system, now the Premier League is exerting its force in relation to the Elite Player Performance Plan (EPPP) and withholding £5m per season to the Football League for Youth development. EPPP will probably lead to a lot of clubs pulling out of having a youth system altogether as the elite s will now pinch other clubs' best players for a much lower fee for players under the age of 17.

Down throughout the Premier League to the Football League pyramid, into non-league and finally into the amateur game at all levels the spiral is complete as the rich get richer and football at the grassroots becomes the major casualty.

At this moment Sport England is cutting £1.6m to the FA for its failure to increase the number of people playing football for fun. The number of 16 year olds and over playing has gone down from 2.02 million to 1.84 million since 2005. Probably disillusioned with the game which might have promised so much in early youth and emulation of Professional Footballers, to the reality of playing on Park pitches with abysmal facilities. This is the biggest issue facing the grass roots game.

Sixty years ago I changed in an air-raid shelter and played on a pitch with scrub grass on it. Today it does not seem as if we have progressed much, considering the standard of living most of us have with computers, mobiles, video games and high speed transport.

A Sky Sports survey in 2014 paints a dismal picture of football in England below academy level with poor facilities, poor pitches and lack of investment in those who play the game and those who run these clubs. Local clubs feel that the FA does not do enough to preserve grassroots football and that the local councils do not do enough to maintain pitches and facilities. So before the FA and governing bodies start harping on about the wonderful facilities at St George's in Burton Upon Trent, remember that the footballing stars of the future will start playing at grassroots football first and they need more care and attention at an early age than glorifying a State of the Art facilities which most youngsters will never use or even see.

As I am writing this England have just gone out of the World Cup in Brazil at the group stage. The squad was selected from no more than 66 English players, who were playing regularly in the English Premier and Championship Leagues. Like Paul Scholes of Manchester United fame I consider that we are going to be relegated to the lower streams of international football alongside the rest of the United Kingdom's International sides. Surely this is a detriment to all those 'Coaches' who talk about getting them young and giving them the best chances to move up the ladder in Professional Football and hopefully into the International arena. Do we really need to start picking out young players at 9 years of age. Do they really need to be shown the right way to play football at this stage of development or should we just let them enjoy playing with their schools and local football clubs for a few more precious years?

They are growing up and maybe missing a lot of opportunities to try other things while moving through primary and secondary school. The dream will still be alive if you are good enough and work hard at the game and surely the talent will still be there as a youngster matures at 14 or 15.

I learnt the game from watching Bolton Wanderers and the stars like Nat Lofthouse and then going back to the park and practising the skills I had seen performed endlessly, always dreaming the dream of becoming a footballer.

When I finally moved up to play at Manchester City I was told to learn from what I saw from my peers and to emulate them. Practice and more practice was the order of the day and coaching was putting the skills you had into a team performance. You learned the hard way or you fell by the wayside.

At grassroots in the modern game we should be able to give our young up and coming players good surfaces to practise and play on. Primary and secondary schools should all have a multi-purpose 3G pitch which should be free to the community and not a facility which thriving young football clubs have to pay to use.

The game has moved on and society has also. The youngsters of today live in a society which puts a value on more materialistic possessions than the austerity I was brought up in. Ipso facto we have the football and the footballers we have been brainwashed with by television and advertisers and therefore no better than we deserve.

The difference in the modern day idiom is well stated by Alan Bennett's headmaster in the play *Forty Years On* where he bemoans the death of the England he loved and the traditional English values he cherished.

Once we had a romantic conception of patriotism, chivalry and duty. But it was a duty which didn't have much to do with justice, social justice anyway. The crowd has found the door into the secret garden. Now they will tear up the flowers by the roots, strip the borders and strew them with paper and broken bottles.

In Brazil Roy Hodgson asked his England players to sing the National Anthem with enthusiasm before each game, trying to renew the spirit which was there in 1966. Has the beautiful game passed us by? I feel it may have done so.

The park is still there for the young boy who wishes to dream of football and scoring goals to the roar of the crowd. To the boy I say, never lose sight of your ambition. Pursue the dream because even in today's modern game the chance is always there for the young boy who wants to play football to live the dream as I did.

In the words of my Uncle Bill, "The game we all play is life, and life is just a game". In our case this was always football.

To paraphrase the words of Omar Khayyam *the moving finger has written and now moves on and all our piety and wit cannot lure it back to cancel half a line, nor all our tears wash out a word of it.*

AFTERWORD

Fratres in aeternum

In December 2014 when this book was completed it is important to look at the past and realise that it is 100 years since the start of World War One in which my grandfather fought, and 75 years since the start of World War Two that my Father and Uncles fought in and 70 years since the D-Day landings in Normandy.

My family loved football and throughout the last century Bolton Wanderers, Altrincham FC and later all the clubs I played for including the City Clubs of Manchester and York were at the focal point of discussions in our household. They were even taken into the Theatre of War in 1939 where I am sure football stories were a solace to them away from home.

My story started in the park and I finished it in the park but this brought back melancholy and poignant thoughts of the past. I realise I was very lucky to have an uncle to play football with in the park as many young boys will have had to grow up without a dad or uncle to play football with.

As a eulogy to my Uncle Bill who passed away eight years ago in 2006, my granddaughter Calista wrote a poem that is worth adding to this narrative as a tribute to those who did not come back from wars defending our Country, and to the ones who were lucky enough to return.

"multis fratribus simul in aeternum"

A Soldier's Life

He was one of four brothers,
The youngest at that.
They all went to war,
They all returned back.
He rode out in bravery
On his horse of great pride.
The clatter of hooves,
Remained with him for life.
The Yeomanry were joined,
With the Somerset regiments,
He had a choice between tanks or signals.
He chose signals and life,
As many tanks went to their death.
His brothers were sworn to protect him,
And that they certainly did.
They took the blame for all his mischief,
And stood by him as brothers do,
They all returned safely,
On the bitter, frosty Winters day,
The band of brothers, together for ever.
But those were the days when there were four,
However sadly they exist no more.

For Bill,
"videre in mane"

ACKNOWLEDGEMENTS

David Batters. (1939-2014). York City club historian. York City.
A Complete Record.

David Conn (author) The Beautiful Game?
Searching for the Soul of Football.

Dave Flett. York Evening Press Archives.

Colin Schindler (author) George Best and 21 Others.

Football League Archives 1888-2014.

Football Association Archives 1863-2014.

Wikipedia.org.

York City Football Club.

York Literature Festival Terry Kay and Miles Salter.

Manchester City Football Club. Mike Summerbee.

INDEX

A

B

C

Calvert, Cliff. P174. P200. P206. P211.

Cantona, Eric. P31.

Cappellini, P115.

Capello, Fabio P115.

Carr, Jim. P78.

Cashley, Ray. P201.

Cave, Mickey. P197. P198. P204. P215. P217.

Charles, John. P38. P117. P233.

Charlton, Bobby. P40. P76.

Charlton, Jack. P117. P121.

Chassen, Road. P12. P13. P16. P48. P70. P75.

Chiefs, Atlanta. P92. P94. P95. P99. P180. P185.

Chilton, Chris. P124. P167.

Chivers, Martin. P79.

City, Manchester. P9. P11. P17-P106.

City York. P128-P219. P228.

Clarke, Alan. P121.

Clarke, Clive. P164.

Clay, John. P24. P26. P41. P43. P46. P85.

Clayton, Ronny. P40.

Clemence, Ray. P215.

Clough, Brian. P123. P179. P192.

Colebridge, Clive. P78.

Coleman, Tony. P85-88. P94-96. P98. P180.

Collins, Bobby. P233.

Collins, Doug. P225. P227. P228.

Cowan, Frank. P78.

Craig, Douglas. P169.

Crawford, Graeme. P130. P175. P187. P188. P191. P193. P194. P197. P206. P207.P215. P224.

Crescent, Bootham. P165. P170. P176. P177. P182. P184. P185. P191 – P195. P197. P198. P200. P202. P205. P207. P215. P228.

Cross, Graham. P81.

Crossan Johnny. PP45. P75. P77. P78. P79. P81. P86.

College, Eton. PX1.

Connor, David. P27. P43. P45. P46. P52. P69. P71. P75. P83. P84. P93. P96. P180.

D

E

F

Ford, Fred. P114. P116. P118. P119. P122. P123. P124. P125. P221.

Forgan, Tommy. P172.

Forsyth, Bruce. P189.

Frizzell, Jimmy. P125. P126. P127.

Frost, Ron. P26. P41. P43.

Fulham, FC. P124. P199. P200. P205. P206. P215.

Furnell, Jim. P113.

G

Gardner ,Peter. P77. P84.

Gibson, Dave. P80.

Gillies, Matt. P80.

Ginulfi, Alberto. P115.

Godwin, Harry. P15. P16. P18. P19. P21. P25. P35. P40. P44. P45. P47. P49. P69. P70. P106.

Goodfellow, Jimmy P80.

Gorton, West. P29.

Gorton FC. P29.

Gough, Alistair. P2

Graham, Eve. P51. P52.

Gray, Eddy. P38. P233.

Grey, Matt. P79.

Greaves, Jimmy. P12. P117.

Green, Alderman Norman. P168.

Green, Roger. P89.

Greenhoff, Jimmy. P38.

Griffiths, Walter. P44. P47. P103. P106.

Grummit,t Peter. P75. P76.

H

Harland, Stan. P113. P116. P124.

Hateley, Tony. P86.

Hall, Bredbury. P51.

Hall, Marbury. P34.

Hanover 96. P84.

Harris, Gerry. P51. P52.

I

Leivers, Bill. P30. P36.

Levant, Cup. P4.

Lister, Ian. P96.

Little, Syd. P51.

Liverpool, F C. P5. P214. P215. P234.

Lloyd, Cliff. P229. P230. P231.

Lofthouse, Nat P5. P9. P240.

Longhurst, David. P205.

Lorimer, Peter. P38. P121. P233.

Lydda, Palestine. P4.

Lyons, Barry. P75. P171. P175. P176. P179. P181. P187. P188. P193. P194. P199. P201. P202. P203. P205. P207. P211. P213. P222.

Lynch, Kenny. P51

M

Macari, Lou. P208.

Mackay, Dave. P122. P123. P124. P125. P127.

Mackin, John. P1131

Macrae, Keith. P185. P187.

Madden, Peter. P222. P223. P224. P225. P227. P229. P232.

Maine Road. P17. P18. P20. P23. P25. P27. P28. P31-P40. P42-P46. P71. P75. P78. P79. P80. P89. P102. P185. P186. P188.

Marks, Saint. P29.

Marks, Frank. P168.

Marr, Andrew. P183.

Marsh, Rodney. P1185. P187. P188.

Matthews, Stanley. P1. P40.

McAlinden, Bobby. P25. P26. P42. P43.

McBride, Peter. P43.

McDermott, John. P

McDougall, Ted. P203.

McDowall, Les. P45.

McEwan, Jimmy. P128.

McGuiness, Wilf. P204. P206. P207. P209. P210. P211. P216. P217.

McKenzie, Scott. P98.

McKinlay, Bob. P75.

McLeod, Angus. P210. P211.

McMahon, Kevin. P154.

McMordie, Eric. P212. P2134.

Meadows, Jimmy. P180

Meldrum, Colin. P165. P166. P170. P176. P181. P182. P190. P193. P198. P203.

Melia, Jimmy. P79.

Mellor, Peter. P200. P205. P206.

Mercer, Joe. P48. P73. P75. P76. P77. P82. P85. P86. P88. P89. P93. P94. P98. P99. P102. P104. P105. P106. P109.

Mersey. Valley Trail. P8

Mills, Gary. P170.

Mollatt, Ron. P233.

Morecambe, Eric. P92.

Morgan, Willy. P207.

Moss Side. P18. P19. P186.

Moore, Bill. P128.

Moore, Bobby. P48. P199. P200. P205. P206.

Mulcaster, Richard. PX1.

Mulhearn, Ken. P96. P178. P179.

Mullery, Alan. P200.

Mundy, Jimmy. P96.

Murray, Jimmy. P43. P44. P45.

McGregor, William. PX1.

Matthews, Stanley. P1. P40.

Mitten, Charley. P5.

N

Navarro, Ruben. P91.

Neenan, Joe. P228.

Neilson, Dick. P16. P26. P35.

Newbolt, Sir Henry. P6.

Noble, Bobby. P24. P43.

Noble, Peter. P114. P115. P118. P119. P122. P123. P125.

Nocturnes, Les. P51.

North American Soccer League, NASL. P91.

Norwich City. P118. P120. P125. P203.

O

Oakes, Alan . P45. P46. P76. P77. P92. P93. P111.
Ogden, Chris. P194.
Ogley, Alan. P26. P34. P43. P75. P77. P81.
Oliver, Peter. P197.
O'Loughlin. Nigel. P231.
Osgood, Peter. P232.
Owen Bobby. P102. P103. P105. P106. P223
Owen, Terry. P224.

P

Paine, Terry. P79.
Park, Burnden. P5. P208. P213.
Park, Roker. P202.
Parton, Jeff P125.
Paul, Lynn. P52.
Pardoe, Glyn. P9. P17. I P24. P26. P28. P33. P36. P42. P43. P75. P77. P78. P93. P96. P184.
Partridge, Pat. P212.
Peachey, John. P174. P178. P179. P184. P187.
Peacock, Denis. P231.
Peacock, Keith. P23.
Pearson, Stuart. P202.
Pele, P81. P92.
Penman, Willy. P110. P165.
Peronace, Gigi. P117. P118.
Pollard, Brian. P167. P174. P179. P182. P187. P193. P201. P205. P210. P211.
Potter, Ray. P69.
Poyser, George. P22. P37. P40. P44. P166.
Premier League P5. P234-P237.
Provan, Andy. P121.
Puskas, Ferenc. P64. P65.

Q

R

Rafferty, Kevin. P225.

Ratcliffe, Fred. P223.

Revie, Don. P38. P121. P233.

Richards, John. P188.

Rimmer, Jimmy. P43.

Robson, Sir Bobby. P91. P92.

Robson, Bryan. P236.

Rochdale, FC. P35. P190. P223. P224. P225. P227. P228. P229. P230. P231. P232.

Rogers, Don. P42. P107. P109. P112. P115. P118. P119. P124. P125. P126.

Rooney, Wayne. P236.

Rose, Sidney. P87. P88. P89. P216.

Rovers, Bristol. P191. P192.

Rovers, Doncaster. P221. P222. P225. P231.

Rusholme, Harry. P169.

Rutter, Bert. P168.

S

Sadler, David. P32. P42. P43.

Salvori, Elvio. P115

Sarafand, Palestine. P4.

Scaife, Bob. P229. P232.

Schiller, Paul. P116.

Scholes, Paul. P240.

Seal, Jimmy. P165. P166. P170. P171. P175. P177. P179. P185. P190. P192. P193. P197. P198. P199. P201. P202. P203. P208. P213. P214. P215. P217. P219. P228. P230. P232.

Shaw, David. P126.

Shawcross, David. P36. P47.

Shilton, Peter. P80. P215.

Shinton, Bobby. P128. P130. P131.

Sinclair, Jackie. P80.

Tiffany's. P51.

Topping, Chris. P131. P173. P175. P187. P188. P193. P196. P201. P212. P213. P215.

Top of the Pops. P51.

Toure, Yaya. P235. P236.

Towers, Tony. P187.

Town, Swindon. P107-P127.

Town , Huddersfield. P121. P182. P193. P218. P219. P220.

Trafford, Old. P8. P38. P207. P208.

Trautmann, Bert.P27. P33. P34. P35. P39. P69. P83. P

Trollope, John. P110. P111. P119. P120.

U

United, Manchester. P8. P9. 21. P20. P21. P22. P26. P30. P33. P38. P39. P41. P42. P43. P197. P202. P204. P207. P208.

United, Sheffield. P32. P175.

V

Vava. P91.

Verdin, Major. P4

W

Wagstaffe, David. P36.

Wagstaffe, Ken. P124. P167.

Walker, Ron. P76.

Walsall, FC. P127. P128. P129. P132.

Wann, Dennis. P124. P197. P212. P215. P227. P232.

Wanderers, Bolton. P4. P8. P9. P19. P23. P207. P213.

Waller, Edmund. PX.

Westwood, Eric P34.

Wheldon, Ken. P128. P129. P177.

White, Noel. P5. P234.

Whittle, Maurice. P194. P195.

Wignall, Frank P75.

Wilberforce, Mr. Justice. P44.

Wild, David. P26. P43.

Wilkins, Ray. P49.
Williams, Danny. P107. P109-P113. P121.
With, Peter. P232.
Wolter, Horst. P232.
Wood, Alf. P24. P43.
Wood, Ian. P178.
Wood, Jack. P180.
Woosnam, Max. P32.
Woosnam, Phil. P95. P99.
Woodward, John. P172. P174. P176. P187. P193. P198. P213.
Worthington, Nigel. P180.
Wright, Billy. 1.
Wright, J.F.P152.

X

Y

Yeomanry, Cheshire Regiment. P3. P53-P55.
Yorath, Terry. P233.
Young, Neil. P75. P77. P78. P86. P93. P94. P96. P98.

Z